Dan Liebke is a comedy writer, who was a regular contributor to *MAD Magazine* in Australia for two decades before coming to his senses and turning his comic focus to cricket. In addition to a social media presence on Bluesky (@liebcricket.com), Dan has contributed articles making fun of cricket and cricketers to a variety of magazines and websites (including his own – liebcricket.com). He also co-hosts both the *Can't Bowl, Can't Throw* and *Ridiculous Ashes* cricket podcasts, and has written numerous cricket books, most of which have been published by Affirm Press (including *The 50 Greatest Matches in Australian Cricket*, *The 50 Greatest Australian Cricketers* and *The 100 Funniest Moments in Australian Cricket*, among others). Dan is a genuine all-rounder, equally inept with both bat and ball – and he steadfastly believes that cricket is the funniest, and hence best, sport that humanity has ever invented.

Alex Bowden is a cricket (and cycling) writer who has previously contributed serious, semi-serious and far-from-serious articles to *The Wisden Cricketer*, *Wisden Cricket Monthly* and Wisden.com, as well as *Wisden*'s quarterly publication, *The Nightwatchman*. Somehow or other, he has never actually written for *Wisden* itself. He has, however, also written for several non-*Wisden*-branded cricket publications, such as *ESPNcricinfo*, *Cricket365* and the *Mumbai Mirror*, as well as his own website, *King Cricket* (kingcricket.co.uk), where he has spent the last twenty years wilfully evading all the big stories while covering the England team. Alongside this, he co-hosts the *Ridiculous Ashes* podcast with Dan Liebke – in large part because Dan has displayed a willingness to call him Alex, rather than King Cricket, which he assures you is a quite excruciating nom de plume to inadvertently land yourself with.

THE 50 MOST RIDICULOUS ASHES MOMENTS

DAN LIEBKE & ALEX BOWDEN

affirm press

First published in Australia in 2025 by Affirm Press,
a Simon & Schuster (Australia) Pty Limited company
Bunurong/Boon Wurrung Country
28 Thistlethwaite Street, South Melbourne VIC 3205

Affirm Press is located on the unceded land of the Bunurong/Boon Wurrung peoples of the Kulin Nation. Affirm Press pays respect to their Elders past and present.

New York Amsterdam/Antwerp London Toronto Sydney/Melbourne New Delhi
Visit our website at www.simonandschuster.com.au

AFFIRM PRESS and design are trademarks of Affirm Press Pty Ltd, Inc., used under licence by Simon & Schuster, LLC.

10 9 8 7 6 5 4 3 2 1

© Dan Liebke and Alex Bowden 2025

All rights reserved. No part of this publication may be reproduced, stored in a retrieval system, or transmitted in any form or by any means, electronic, mechanical, photocopying, recording or otherwise, without prior permission of the publisher.

The moral rights of the authors have been asserted.

9781923135697 (paperback)
9781761639746 (ebook)

Cover design by Luke Causby/Blue Cork
Cover photograph by Mike Egerton/PA Images/Alamy Stock Photo
Typeset by Post Pre-press Group in 10/15 pt Garamond Premier Pro
Printed and bound in China by C&C Offset Printing Co., Ltd

Dan:
For Kris and Nathan, brothers and worthy backyard cricket opponents

Alex:
For Dad for cricket and Mum for words

CONTENTS

A REAL FOREWORD FROM THE REAL PAT CUMMINS 1
A PERHAPS NOT-QUITE-SO-REAL FOREWORD FROM AN ANONYMOUS 39-YEAR-OLD FORMER ENGLAND MEDIUM PACER 2
INTRODUCTION 3

50 SHANE WARNE CONSOLES HIMSELF WITH AN IMPERFECT HAT-TRICK 4
49 GERAINT JONES MAKES A PAIR 10
48 BEN STOKES TRIES TO REINVENT TEST CRICKET 16
47 THE WOMEN CELEBRATE FIFTY YEARS OF TEST CRICKET 22
46 THE CENTENARY TEST 28
45 ENGLAND SLIP INTO THE NINETIES 34
44 PETER TAYLOR MAKES HIS DEBUT 40
43 THE LONGEST DAY IN THE HISTORY OF TEST CRICKET 46
42 TERRY ALDERMAN'S SECOND-MOST PRODUCTIVE ASHES SERIES 52
41 MITCHELL JOHNSON BOWLS NEITHER TO THE LEFT NOR TO THE RIGHT 58
40 ENGLAND FALL APART 64
39 90S 99S, REPRISE 70
38 ROOT AND PAINE SUCCESSFULLY OVERTURN DECISIONS … BUT WITH MIXED RESULTS 76
37 ENGLAND REFUSE TO TAKE WICKETS 82
36 ENGLAND'S CUNNING PLAN 88
35 MARK TAYLOR REFUSES A GIFT 94
34 CAPTAINCY '81 100
33 BETH MOONEY TAKES A CHANCE 106
32 STEVE WAUGH HAS A HEADACHE 112
31 JAMES VINCE SUCCESSFULLY AVOIDS NICKING ONE FROM MITCHELL STARC 118

30	ALLAN BORDER AND JEFF THOMSON FALL SHORT	124
29	A ZILLION RUNS AT THE GABBA	130
28	NAT SCIVER-BRUNT SCORES A RESULT-ALTERING TON	136
27	NASSER ASKS AUSTRALIA TO BAT	142
26	ENGLAND LACK WHEELS	148
25	AUSTRALIA CELEBRATE A DRAW	154
24	MICHAEL SLATER IS RUN OUT BUT NOT OUT	160
23	STUART BROAD'S FINAL ACTS	166
22	CHRIS ROGERS IS LBW TO GRAEME SWANN	172
21	ENGLAND PICK THE SAME TEAM	178
20	STEVE SMITH REVIEWS AND WALKS FOR AN LBW	184
19	SARAH TAYLOR'S SLIP FIELDING	190
18	STEVE WAUGH BATS WITH ONE LEG	196
17	WHEN STUART BROAD FAILED TO DISMISS EXTRAS AT TRENT BRIDGE	202
16	STEVE HARMISON BOWLS A WIDE	208
15	90S 99S	214
14	ASHTON AGAR DOES SOMETHING UNEXPECTED	220
13	A RUN-OUT STEALS THE SHOW	226
12	AUSTRALIA'S OPENERS ARE RUN OUT (× 6)	232
11	ENGLAND'S HEAD START	238
10	ELLYSE PERRY PERFORMS FEATS OF HYPERCOMPETENCE	244
9	JIMMY AND MONTY SAVE ENGLAND	250
8	JONNY BAIRSTOW LEAVES HIS GROUND	256
7	AMAZING ADELAIDE, THE TEST THAT NEVER HAPPENED	262
6	SHANE WATSON IS DISMISSED	268
5	STOKES THE HEADINGLEY HERO	274
4	IAN BOTHAM PERFORMS LUDICROUS FEATS OF HEROISM	282
3	STUART BROAD SMASHES ONE TO SLIP	288
2	GERAINT JONES CATCHES MICHAEL KASPROWICZ	294
1	SHANE WARNE SHOWS UP	302

| ACKNOWLEDGEMENTS | 309 |
| IMAGE CREDITS | 310 |

A REAL FOREWORD FROM THE REAL PAT CUMMINS

As an Ashes-winning (and, yes, retaining) captain, I know that cricket – especially Ashes cricket – can be ridiculous. Shane Warne's ball of the century. A teenage Ashton Agar coming in at number eleven and scoring 98 on debut. Scott Boland's 6/7. All good, silly stuff.

Even more ridiculous, the whole purpose of these matches is to win an old bail that somebody once decided to set on fire.

Of course, no matter whether we win the series 5–0, or 4–0, or 2–2, the Marylebone Cricket Club never actually hands over the physical urn that contains the Ashes. They say we can't be trusted with it (probably fair).

So really what we Australians compete for is the *idea* of a burnt bail that symbolises the death of English cricket – which, if I'm not mistaken, has actually lived on for well over a century since that bail was incinerated.

Maybe it's best not to dissect it too much. All I know is that both teams are sufficiently motivated that it can feel pretty intense out there and ridiculous on-field events frequently ensue.

But how ridiculous, exactly? Well, that's what Dan and Alex have sorted out.

Will that time Nathan Lyon and I put on an unbeaten 55-run ninth-wicket partnership to win the first Test in 2023 be the No. 1 moment? No, probably not. Still. Fun to remember, right?

A PERHAPS NOT-QUITE-SO-REAL FOREWORD FROM AN ANONYMOUS 39-YEAR-OLD FORMER ENGLAND MEDIUM PACER[1]

Ashes cricket, ridiculous? Is it? Is it really?

Sure, the odd England batter's looked a little ridiculous when they've been rapped on the pad by a flipper when playing for a leg-break. But is that really any more ridiculous than a hard-handed Aussie edging to slip after multiple teammates have already fallen the exact same way on the first morning of a Test?

And maybe walking for an LBW is ridiculous. But is it honestly any more ridiculous than failing to walk after smashing one straight to slip? And would that become more or less ridiculous if 'straight to slip' in fact meant 'indirectly to slip as a consequence of a deflection off the wicketkeeper'?

Or what about a tailender spending half an eternity demanding that the position of a sightscreen be endlessly fine-tuned? Is that really so ludicrous? Surely, with less actual skill to make use of, a tailender is more vulnerable to distraction than a top-order batter. If anything, the shorter an innings ultimately proves to be, the more time should previously have been invested in sightscreen manipulation.

Is the Ashes ridiculous? If these things prove anything, it is only that the Ashes is an extremely big deal indeed.

There really is very little that is ridiculous about dedicating your whole life towards claiming temporary shared ownership of the idea of a burnt bail that symbolises the death of English cricket, and shame on Alex and Dan for suggesting otherwise.

---

1   Identity withheld by request of *The Courier-Mail* newspaper (see No. 3).

INTRODUCTION

The phrase 'you know it when you see it' traces back at least as far as *The Hound of the Baskervilles*, written by Sir Arthur Conan Doyle (first-class statistics: ten matches, 231 runs at 19.25), in which Sherlock Holmes passes implicit judgement on a portrait by claiming, 'I know what is good when I see it.'

The phrase was further popularised in 1964 by United States Supreme Court justice Potter Stewart (first-class statistics: zero matches, zero runs), when he decreed that while he might not be able to 'intelligibly' define the kinds of material that would be considered pornographic, he knew it when he saw it.

As it goes with fictional portraiture and mid-20th-century dirty movies, so it goes with ridiculous cricket. Arguably, the most delightful aspect of this great sport is its propensity to throw forth ridiculousness when you least expect it, and often with little relationship to the quality of the cricket being played. We can have ridiculously good cricket or ridiculously bad cricket. Or, just as often, ridiculously ridiculous cricket. We may not be able to intelligibly define why a moment qualifies or why it doesn't, but regardless of the form it takes, we know it when we see it.

Cricket is the greatest sport humankind has ever invented. Test cricket is its pinnacle. The Ashes is where it all began. And ridiculous cricket is the best kind of cricket. It therefore follows that ridiculous Ashes cricket is something to treasure and, for the purposes of this book, rank.

So let's count down the fifty most ridiculous Ashes moments.[1]

---

1   Of the last fifty years. We're not going to get bogged down in Bradman's statistical ridiculousness, which, while undeniably top-tier nonsense, is also, ultimately, too dull to bother with.

50

SHANE WARNE CONSOLES HIMSELF WITH AN IMPERFECT HAT-TRICK

AKA PHIL TUFNELL, ESCAPOLOGIST

Leg-spin is a famously difficult art. Why even bother? Well, the rewards are so much greater, aren't they? Not in the sense of taking more wickets necessarily, but often in the quality of the ones you do take.

Because while any style of bowler can hit a batter's stumps from time to time, only a wrist spinner can make the victim look like they've never held a cricket bat before.

Shane Warne dismissed Alec Stewart fourteen times in Test cricket. Most people look a bit substandard when they're losing their wicket – that's the natural dynamic of the moment, really – but on one of those fourteen occasions Warne succeeded in making Stewart look like a person who was not a professional cricketer.

The moment came in the fourth innings of the first Test of the 1994/95 Ashes. England were looking to bat out time, midway through the fourth day, having been set an impossible 508 to win. Opening the batting with Mike Atherton, Stewart had started well. He was on 29 and England had yet to lose a wicket.

Warne bowled a leg break. It was a bit short and Stewart moved back and cut it for four. That brought up the 50. Things were looking ... well, not great overall, let's be honest, but okay considering how the rest of the match had gone.

It was a nice shot and a nice little landmark. A moment or two later, when Warne ambled in and bowled the next one, Stewart watched the ball closely and thought that the delivery was exactly the same.

Alas for Stewart, this delivery was not exactly the same.

It would be wrong to say that Stewart again played a cut shot, even though that's how everyone remembers it. The truth is he raised his bat and positioned his feet to play a cut, but then the stroke he actually played was an underpants-smearingly panicked leg swish. It was a truly horrible shot, the kind of filthy swipe across the line that is routinely unfurled by a four-year-old who insists on standing facing the bowler, rather than adopting the side-on stance the textbook recommends.

What had happened was that Shane Warne had bowled a flipper instead of a leg break. It had been short, yes, but rather than languidly turning away from Stewart and looping up to a nice, hittable spot, it had instead zooted through, quick and straight, splattering the stumps while his bat was still on the way down.

Rarely does a top-order Test match batter look this bad, because Test match

Shane Warne flips off Alec Stewart.

batters rarely misread exactly where and when the ball will arrive quite so badly. It was, in all honesty, the definitive example of what a flipper can do. And Warne was only getting started.

He finished with 8/71 that innings and was at one point a whisker[1] away from taking a hat-trick with three entirely different deliveries when his intended piece de resistance wrong'un beat both Phil Tufnell (easily) and the stumps (very, very narrowly).

The ball before that, Martin McCague had succeeded in looking less silly to a flipper than Stewart but had still been dismissed by it. The one before that had been a fiercely spun leg break that hit Phil DeFreitas's stumps.

The DeFreitas wicket was actually the most ludicrous of all. Despite planting his front foot on leg stump, he was bowled behind his legs by a ball delivered from over the wicket that landed pretty much on a yorker length.

Just take a moment to consider the physics of that. Even multiple slow-motion replays didn't make what happened seem credible.

Three balls, three wholly different deliveries and almost – *almost* – a wicket with each. Really, with hindsight, this was a level of ridiculousness that has only ever been accessible to Shane Warne.

His failure to dismiss Tufnell did, however, mean that at this point in his career, he had never taken a hat-trick – even as a junior.[2]

In the first innings of the second Test, he failed again and had to settle for 6/64. The tourists then collapsed so rapidly to Damien Fleming and Craig McDermott in their second innings that by the time they were 6/91, Warne didn't have a single wicket to his name – let alone three from consecutive deliveries.

No matter. DeFreitas was LBW for 0, then Darren Gough was caught behind for 0 to set up a second hat-trick opportunity in two Tests.

Now, if you were Shane Warne, who would you most want to see walking to the crease for another go at a hat-trick ball? The answer was Tufnell, obviously. He'd missed the previous hat-trick ball by a mile. This was a man who would finish his Test career with a batting average of 5.10.

---

1   An appropriate margin, really, given the batter's nickname of 'The Cat'.
2   Not ordinarily a remarkable fact, a 'failure' to secure hat-tricks – but this was Shane Warne.

Alas, Tufnell was batting in his customary position at number eleven, so Warne had to contend with the extra competence of a number ten.

Only two batters ever came in after Tufnell in Test cricket. One was Ed Giddins, who only played four Tests, none of which was in an Ashes series. The other was Devon Malcolm. For this Test at least, Malcolm was considered number ten material.

This may have been a correct assessment, but while Malcolm's final Test career batting average of 6.05 ultimately suggests that he was around 20 per cent better at batting than Tufnell, we're in real 'best-looking deep-sea fish' territory here. 'Most viable number ten' was not a hotly contested title for England in 1994. It was no great surprise when Malcolm inside-edged his first ball to a diving David Boon[3] at short leg.

Warne had his hat-trick. Tufnell was again the one that got away, though. The end of the over provided The Cat with an opportunity to scamper to the other end, where he swiftly secured a duck to McDermott (and a pair for the match).

ACTIVITY CORNER

1. Imagine Phil Tufnell and Devon Malcolm battling to save a Test match with the bat.
2. Just imagine it.

---

3   A hat-trick. Athleticism from David Boon. Quite the occasion!

49

GERAINT JONES MAKES A PAIR

AKA ADAM GILCHRIST EMULATES A MUPPET

Adam Gilchrist does his best to ignore the heckling from Statler and Waldorf.

There are many points of contrast one can make between the 2005 and 2006/07 Ashes. The former is widely considered the greatest Ashes contest ever. The latter was less a contest and more a vengeful obliteration of an England team that had shown the temerity to not just compete in an Ashes series, but to actually win the thing.

In 2005, England, after talking up their chances prior to the first Test, had been left deflated by a Glenn McGrath masterclass (9/82 match figures with the ball, but also, incredibly, 30 undefeated runs with the bat), only to bounce back immediately. England dominated most of the second Test, at Edgbaston, holding off a late Shane Warne–led charge to claim a famous two-run victory.

In 2006/07, England didn't have to talk up their chances prior to the first Test. Every cricket fan in the world had talked up this return Ashes series from the instant the previous one ended. Nevertheless, Australia again dominated the first Test, winning by 277 runs (although McGrath's impact was kept to a mere seven wickets and eight undefeated runs). Once again, however, England bounced back immediately, dominating most of the second Test, at Adelaide, until Shane Warne led an improbable comeback, which this time around England were powerless to repel.[1]

England wicketkeeper Geraint Jones had been a key figure in the climactic moment of the 2005 second Test, as the man who held Michael Kasprowicz's gloved[2] chance off a Steve Harmison short ball to secure the win.

As it had for most of the English players, 2006/07 had gone somewhat less well for Jones. Heading into the third Test, at the WACA, he had not taken a single catch that would be replayed forever as an iconic Ashes moment, for example, and with the bat he'd contributed scores of 19, 33, 1 and 10. These 63 runs in four innings were below expectations for the wicketkeeper-batter, but it could have been worse. He could have made a pair, for example.

Australia batted first, and Jones held a sharp, juggling catch off the

---

1   There'll be much, much more on both these very ridiculous second Tests later in this countdown.
2   If you know, you know.

bowling of Monty Panesar (brought in to replace Ashley Giles, who'd taken an unsatisfactory 3/262 over the first two Tests) to dismiss Andrew Symonds (brought in to replace Damien Martyn, who'd taken an unexpected early retirement after the first two Tests[3]). It was one of three catches for Jones, and one of five wickets for Panesar, as England bowled Australia out late on the first day for 244.

In reply, England could only make 215, with Jones contributing a four-ball duck, slicing Symonds to a diving Justin Langer at point. Nevertheless, with Australia holding just a 29-run first-innings lead and Matthew Hoggard bowling Langer with the first ball of Australia's second innings, there remained a chance that England could fight their way back into the Test, and perhaps even the series.

A day later, those chances had been completely snuffed out. Matthew Hayden had scored 92, Ricky Ponting 75, Mike Hussey 103 and Michael Clarke 79 not out as Australia stretched their lead to just shy of 400. Sure, Symonds had fallen to Panesar again, caught by Paul Collingwood for 2, but this had only brought Adam Gilchrist to the crease.

Gilchrist had made just one more run than his wicketkeeping counterpart, Jones, in the series to that point – although admittedly from two fewer innings, not having been required to bat in the second innings of the first two Tests.

Not batting in the second innings is certainly one way to avoid a pair. Another way, though, is to score the second-fastest century in the history of Test cricket. (Second-fastest at the time, that is. At the time of writing, it is languishing in fourth place.)

Throughout the 2005 Ashes, Gilchrist, the most feared wicketkeeper-batter in the history of the game, had been a non-factor. The England bowlers – notably Andrew Flintoff – had gone around the wicket to the left-hander, cramping his batting and restricting him to 181 runs for the series at 22.62, with a highest score of 49 not out. And although Gilchrist had scored 64 in Adelaide, he'd made ducks in his other two visits to the crease,

---

3 Martyn would eventually explain that he tried to retire before the series began but was talked out of it. So instead he pounced while everybody was still hungover after the Adelaide win, notifying Cricket Australia via email and the captain (and best man at his wedding), Ricky Ponting, via text message while he was playing golf with Stuart Clark.

raising the prospect of another series of limited impact.

Once again, however, the timelines of the two series diverged. In 57 balls of Fozzie Bear-esque WACA whacking, Gilchrist launched his way to a thrilling ton, much to the delight of both his home crowd and a cackling Mark Taylor on commentary. The lead surged to 556 before Ponting displayed a semblance of mercy, calling in Gilchrist and Clarke (who'd made his way to a sluggish-in-comparison 135 not out from 164 balls).

England had two and a bit days to save the Test and keep their chances of retaining the urn technically alive. In the corresponding Test in 2005, Australia had been given one day fewer to survive and had scrambled their way to a draw nine wickets down.

A century from young opener Alastair Cook helped England drag the 2006/07 Test into the final day, and a counterattack from Flintoff and Kevin Pietersen in the first hour even raised brief hopes of the most improbable of victories. But Flintoff's wicket brought Jones to the crease.

Jones was on a pair, just as Gilchrist had been. It was too much, surely, to expect him to emulate Gilchrist's onslaught. Right?

Right.

From the final ball of the first full over he faced, Jones missed a sweep shot and Warne bellowed for an LBW. Jones held his defensive pose, perhaps to show umpire Rudi Koertzen how far down the pitch he'd been when the ball had struck his pad.

This was a good ploy, in the sense that Koertzen gave him not out. It was a less good ploy in the sense that Jones was so far down the pitch that his back foot was outside the crease. Ponting, fielding in close on the off side, noticed this and underarmed the ball into the stumps while everybody else was waiting for Koertzen's decision.

Jones was out for one of the doziest ducks the Ashes had ever seen (run out, in case you're wondering), completing the pair. He was dropped for the fourth Test and never played Test cricket again.

Gilchrist retired at the end of the following summer, having played in 96 consecutive Tests. The 57-ball century was the final one of his Test career.

48

BEN STOKES TRIES TO REINVENT TEST CRICKET

AKA BAZBALL V CUMBALL

Ben Stokes appeals for a slight rewrite of the laws of the game.

'We're trying to rewrite how Test cricket is being played in England,' said Ben Stokes early in his captaincy tenure, following a series of successful run chases of escalating size against New Zealand and India.

When Australia arrived a year later for the 2023 Ashes, the tourists' attitude to Stokes's claim essentially amounted to an eye-rolling, 'Okay ... you do you.'

Because Pat Cummins and his men felt no real motivation to reinvent anything. England may have scored 500 runs on the opening day of an away series against Pakistan a few months earlier, but Australia had just beaten India in the final of the World Test Championship. The feeling was that England's increasingly ludicrous approach to Test batting would almost certainly founder on the rocks of Australian fast bowling.

Whatever the merits of this view, when Zak Crawley larruped the first ball of the series for four, it was clear that England had no intention of tempering their approach. England brought their 100 up in 20 overs, with regular wickets having minimal impact on their scoring rate. Even after falling to 5/176, they pressed on. In the first over after tea, Joe Root reversed his stance and part-scooped, part-walloped Scott Boland for six.

Then, late on that first day, with the score reading 8/393 and Root on 118, having just taken a Nathan Lyon over for 20, Stokes declared. Much bafflement ensued, with the man himself later explaining he had seen it as a 'chance to pounce' on Australia's opening batters, Usman Khawaja and David Warner.

Khawaja, in particular, was not to be pounced upon.

While both Aussie openers survived the four overs remaining on day one, Warner was seemingly inevitably dismissed by Stuart Broad the next morning.[1] Khawaja, though? He saw England's rambunctious, fast-scoring approach, admired it and then politely said, 'No, thank you.'

Where England had scored at five runs an over during their innings, Khawaja made his runs at pretty much exactly half that pace. If England pounced, they pounced over him.

---

[1] Warner had lost his wicket to Broad seven times on the previous Ashes tour and finished that series one Josh Hazlewood single away from having the lowest average of all the Australians.

In a quite magnificent display of not-giving-a-toss-what-anyone-else-has-been-doing, he made 141 runs off 321 balls in eight hours of batting.

Bat for that long and you'll encounter more than your fair share of Ben Stokes captaincy innovations. The most striking of these came early on that second morning.

After two quick wickets to Broad, Australia were 2/39 and, if not on the ropes, then certainly within leaning distance of them. Who did Khawaja and Steve Smith expect to see come on to bowl at this point? Ollie Robinson, most likely. Or perhaps Stokes himself. Maybe even Moeen Ali.

Probably not Harry Brook.

If you have never seen Brook's bowling, you can infer its nature from a couple of comments that were made during that over.

First of all, commentator Mike Atherton saw fit to enquire of Ricky Ponting, 'Who's the filthiest bowler you ever got out to?'

Meanwhile, on the pitch, Jonny Bairstow somehow managed to capture both the nonsense and the left-field threat of what was happening by excitedly needling Smith with, 'Ooh, what's coming next?'

Pure, scintillating part-time military-medium was the answer. At no point in his over did Brook manage to top 110 kilometres per hour.

When the dust eventually settled on the teams' respective first innings, we finally got a sense of the difference between these two sides, with their different approaches, seemingly playing almost different sports. That difference amounted to seven runs in England's favour.

England again stamped on the accelerator and made 273 in their second innings with no one passing fifty and no one much giving the impression such a thing was any great concern.

In reply, Khawaja hit the brakes, slowing his scoring still further to make 65 in over five hours at the crease. Despite this, Australia fell to 8/227 in pursuit of 281 for victory. The jig, if not quite up, was at the very least high and rising.

Cummins and Lyon were at the crease. Criticised for being boring throughout the match, Cummins spent the next half-hour as the central figure in one of the most excruciatingly dramatic passages of Ashes cricket.

For those thirty minutes, the pair employed their seemingly edgeless bats to slot a large number of matter-of-fact runs into the endless green spaces of Edgbaston. The tension ratcheted up and up, and then – Test cricket being Test cricket – carried on ratcheting upwards from there.

At one point Cummins hammered Root for two sixes in an over. He dug out yorkers. He took blows to the body. And then eventually it came. He hit the winning runs and – fundamentally a bowler at heart – discarded his bat in celebration.

'Ice in his veins,' diagnosed Atherton.

Athers neglected to float a suggestion as to what might be within Stokes's veins. Some sort of highly-caffeinated glucose-fructose energy drink, presumably – because England's captain hadn't run out of tricks yet. In the second Test, at Lord's, he attempted to hit back by almost entirely renouncing logic.

The most obvious manifestation of this was when he attempted to reprise his 2019 Headingley innings (spoiler alert: we may return to that one) by having a good old tilt at a fourth-innings victory target of 371 after his side had fallen to 6/193. The fact that his 155 got England within 43 runs of victory should really have been the maddest feature of the match. Yet somehow it wasn't.

England had fielded five right-arm not-that-quick bowlers, with injury absences somehow resulting in Josh Tongue's upper-end-of-fast-medium being talked up as a real unique selling point. Stuart Broad and James Anderson were playing in their final Ashes series, Ollie Robinson was being lambasted by Matthew Hayden for his '124-kilometre-per-hour nude nuts', and Stokes's knee was sufficiently shot that he wouldn't bowl again after this match for almost a year. The captain surveyed the popgun arsenal at his disposal and for some reason concluded: 'Let's bounce them out!'

But not only that, Stokes then stuck to this tactic with a monomania even Captain Ahab would have baulked at. In Australia's second innings, England bowled 98 per cent short balls for 51 overs in a row.

That is one of those statistics that is so ludicrous it can only be perceived as an exaggeration. But no. It is not an exaggeration. That's an actual, genuine statistic. Even more outrageous, England did this with no fast bowlers.

Somehow it worked out for them, because Australia were dismissed for 279. (Allowing Australia to reach 3/316 in the first innings after putting them into bat was where the Test really got away from them.)

So with the game lost and facing a 2–0 deficit, there was surely now a temptation to persist with the medium-pace bounce-a-thon masterplan.

Nope. For the third Test, England instead recalled Mark Wood, whose first spell climaxed with a 152-kilometres-per-hour delivery that flattened Khawaja's leg stump.

Wood took 5/38, England continued scoring at five runs an over, Mitch Marsh forgot what team he was playing for and accidentally made a run-a-ball 118, and at the end of the game the series score was 2–1.

For the fourth Test, at Old Trafford, England sped up, opener Zak Crawley laying waste to the Australian attack in frighteningly untroubled fashion, before Australia retained the Ashes with a draw thanks to rain, rain and Marnus Labuschagne.

There was still another Test to go, though, which gave Stokes the opportunity for one last transcendentally mad moment of captaincy just before lunch on the final day.

Moeen Ali bowled, Steve Smith propped forward and the ball looped in the air to Stokes himself at leg slip. Smith was given not out by the on-field umpires, but Stokes was persuaded to refer the decision to the third umpire.

Had the ball hit Smith's glove? Yes, it had. One small detail, though: Stokes hadn't actually caught it. While he'd successfully grasped the ball initially, it had bounced out of his hand upon landing. Reviewing a catch you haven't actually taken? Stokes tragically failed in his bid to rewrite how Test catches can be taken.

But what of the broader rewrite, of how Test cricket was played? The missed chance didn't stop England securing the victory, which meant that, after a whole series of England nonsense and Australian pragmatism that at times came across as almost wilfully ridiculous, given the way the opposition were behaving, the series ended … all square.

47

THE WOMEN CELEBRATE FIFTY YEARS OF TEST CRICKET

AKA THE BENDIGO BELLY

WELCOME TO BENDIGO
VICTORIA

Home of 1980s fine dining.

When you're asked to think of the most ridiculous Ashes moments, we'll forgive you if the 1984/85 women's Ashes doesn't immediately leap to mind. Which is a shame, because the series, and in particular the second Test, is a secret kitbag stuffed full of cricketing nonsense.

Let's unpack it, shall we, scattering the absurdities all over this entry (which is our messy corner of the dressing room in this rather forced analogy)?

The 1984/85 women's Ashes celebrated fifty years of women's Test cricket, even if it was a half-century not exactly jam-packed with Testy goodness. The previous women's Ashes had taken place almost a decade earlier, in England in 1976, and the last time the England women had toured Australia had been in 1968/69. Furthermore, both those series had consisted of three three-day Tests, which resulted in every match being drawn. England had, however, somehow won a Test during the series prior to those two (in 1963) and, as a result, had held the urn for more than two decades. In your face, Australia men's team of the 1990s and early 2000s!

Enough was enough, though. The 1984/85 series was going to be a proper contest for the urn. For the first (and, as it turned out, only[1]) time, the women's Ashes would consist of five Tests instead of three. They would also be four-day matches. Let's see you finish the series 0–0 this time, ladies.

The England women arrived in Perth to the usual pre-Ashes speculation prior to the match that they would be unable to handle the quicker Australian bowlers. England, for their part, omitted their quickest bowler, Sarah Potter (the daughter of playwright Dennis, and no relation to fictional boy wizard Harry), from the squad, apparently because she had a tendency to dye her hair blue. The selectors denied this was the reason – but then they would, wouldn't they?

Not that it mattered. England had the better of the first Test at the WACA, vindicating the selectors' insistence on a team of traditionally hued hairstyles, but Australia escaped with a draw, eight wickets down and 73 runs short of victory.

---

1 Prove us wrong, CA and ECB!

The climax to that draw was mired in confusion. Australia needed exactly 100 in the last hour to win, but nobody knew how many overs there were to bowl. Initially, it was thought to be twenty. Then that number changed when somebody remembered that both sides had agreed to play 110 overs each day. (Yes, you read that number correctly.)

The England 12th woman came onto the ground three times to discuss the situation with the umpires. (Presumably on behalf of the management, but it is quite fun to imagine a substitute fielder with irresistibly strong opinions on playing conditions for the final hour.) Eventually, it was agreed that play would end at 5.30pm, and England bowled 16 overs in the final hour.

A fun, chaotic start to the series.

Six weeks later, the series ended in similarly chaotic fashion at Queen Elizabeth Oval, in Bendigo. The series was locked at 1–1, and heading into the fourth day Australia held the upper hand. England were 5/140, a lead of just 51, but if they could hold on for a draw they would retain the Ashes.

One small problem, though. Microscopic, even. A virus (swiftly and alliteratively dubbed 'Bendigo belly') had swept (and, in some cases, reverse-swept) through both camps the night before. England had two players incapacitated, Australia three. One umpire also tapped out when the virus struck him down. (There were thoughts that perhaps this was all a bout of food poisoning, but this grave culinary slander was forcefully rebutted in the local media by a perhaps-not-completely-objective Bendigo doctor.)

England batter Jackie Court[2] retired hurt (or possibly sick) early on that disease-riddled final day. She was replaced by the ill Janet Tedstone (nee Aspinall), who was immediately out for a duck, forcing Court to resume batting straightaway. Court was then also out with no further runs added to the score. Eventually, the ailing England side were dismissed for 204, setting the similarly ailing Australia 116 to win.

Australia meandered their way to 0/29 from the first 20 overs – partially because of the slow pitch, but mostly because their number three,

---

2   In a pen portrait of the England squad, Court listed her hobbies as 'mud wrestling, deep sea diving and spending money', so clearly she was a wonderfully silly player.

Jill Kennare, had one of the queasiest tummies, and they were wary of stumbling and collapsing at the final, stomach-buggy hurdle.

But as the day wore on, players recovered and Australia completed a three-wicket win. Everybody then celebrated fifty years of women's Tests by exchanging blazers and drinking champagne, and no doubt by speculating about the previous night's dinner, no matter what that Bendigo quack claimed.

The fourth days of the first and final Tests are, however, merely the slices of nonsense bread surrounding the nuttier-than-Nutella second Test interior of this ridiculous Ashes sandwich. (The third and fourth Tests are a double thickness of boring butter in this analogy, which, yes, is completely different to the one in the opening paragraphs.)

Australia began the second Test with a new captain, police officer Raelee Thomson, after Sharon Tredrea retired, having suffered an Achilles tendon injury in the first Test. They struck early, bowling England out for 91, thanks to Karen Price's fiery spell of 4/22 off 17 overs. A particular highlight of England's batting was the knock from Chris Watmough, who 'steadied the innings', according to match reports at the time, but also 'failed to score' despite spending sixty-nine minutes at the crease.

The first day ended with Australia 1/84, just seven runs in arrears. England captain Jan Southgate 'declined to comment' on her side's performance, and fair enough too. If you can't say something nice …

Australia went on to reach 262, thanks primarily to opener Denise Emerson (sister of Terry Alderman and wife of umpire Ross Emerson), who made 121, despite having chipped a bone in her thumb while fielding. England scored 296 in their second innings – and here's where things began to get utterly mad.

Australia had most of the fourth day to reach the 126 they needed to win. But Southgate set aggressive fields. As she said after the match, 'We really didn't have any option. We certainly couldn't have won from our position if we had spread out the field and tried to save runs.' She also said after the match, 'The English are a race that don't panic – and we weren't panicking out there,' so it's great to know that it's not just the men who can talk press conference bollocks.

The aggressive fields and sharp catching saw left-arm spinner Gillian McConway and medium pacer Avril

Starling[3] destroy the Australian top order, reducing them to 5/6. (In wicketty starts to innings, we're aware scoreboard confusion can sometimes arise. Obviously, 5/6 is dreadful no matter which way around it is, but, to be clear, this was five wickets down and only six runs scored.)

It was somehow even worse than that, however. Australia's last three wickets in the first innings had also fallen for no runs. So this second-innings collapse completed a run of eight wickets lost for just six runs.

The remaining 120 runs needed for victory could not have looked further away. But Karen Price and Lyn Fullston commenced the fightback. They added 67 for the sixth wicket, before new captain Thomson and the rest of the tail then chipped in to get Australia within a shot of victory. McConway and Starling then prised out the final two wickets. A stunning fourth-day collapse had allowed a ridiculous comeback win to England by just five runs.

And that's why you don't limit Test matches to three days.

---

3   Surely one of the first cricketers to be christened via social media name generator. In this instance, the first name of your favourite female, Canadian, pop-punk singer from the early 2000s, followed by the next bird that you see.

46

THE CENTENARY TEST

AKA WHAT A DIFFERENCE A CENTURY MAKES

Let's get the awkward fact out of the way first: the Centenary Test between Australia and England was not technically an Ashes match. However, the mere notion that Test cricket between those two teams could be anything other than the Ashes seems sufficiently ridiculous that it surely warrants inclusion in this book, right?

Right?

Well, it's in. What are you going to do? Tear a few pages out? Change the 50 on the cover to 49? Seems like a lot of work.

The idea was that 100 years of Test cricket should be marked with a game between the same two teams who played the very first Test (Australia and England), at the very same ground (the MCG[1]). So that's what they did.

The 1877 Test had been a colourful one. England's first-choice wicketkeeper, Ted Pooley, was unavailable for selection as he was in jail in New Zealand following a betting scandal earlier in the tour. Their second choice, Harry Jupp, was suffering sufficiently inflamed eyes that he wasn't trusted to keep wicket – so they asked him to open the batting instead, where he top-scored in the first innings.[2]

Australia had selection issues too. Fred Spofforth refused to play because he felt like the wrong wicketkeeper had been picked, only for his replacement, Frank Allan, to also pull out in favour of going to a local fair. So far, so Springfield Isotopes-esque.

The match is best remembered for the unmatched feat of Charles Bannerman, who not only faced the first ball in Test cricket, but then proceeded to set a record that is still to be broken in men's matches: the greatest percentage of a team's innings total scored by a single batter. Bannerman's 165 not out constituted 67.3 per cent of Australia's eventual 245.[3] He retired hurt with a finger injury.

England were then bowled out for 196, before dismissing Australia for 104 in the second innings. They were back in it, but chasing 154 to win, they

---

1   The first match was originally scheduled to be played at the East Melbourne Cricket Ground, which would have been less convenient a hundred years later, given the EMCG closed in 1921.
2   He is said to have trodden on his wicket on 0 but neither umpire noticed. Alas, TV replays had not yet been invented, what with TV not having yet been invented either.
3   Bannerman had made 126 out of 6/166 at the end of the first day, at which point both teams apparently went to the opera.

could only make 108,[4] meaning that Australia won by 45 runs. Remember that margin, kids! (Everyone else, maybe write it down. Your memory's not what it was, is it? Let's be honest.)

Fast-forward to the futuristic year of 1977 and England arrived in Australia on their somewhat circuitous way home from a Test tour of India, where they'd triumphed 3–1.

The 1877 Test had been a 'timeless' one, with no set finish. The 1977 one was scheduled for five days, but that seemed optimistic when England responded to Australia's 138 with 95 all out, before reducing the home team to 3/53.[5]

The game was played in March and it was cloudy and damp in the preceding days. Australia captain Greg Chappell reckoned it 'probably came about 36 hours too soon for the pitch'.

Australia opener Rick McCosker had been among the first to misjudge the bounce, suffering the insult-to-injury fate of being bowled by Bob Willis after the ball had deflected off both his hand and his jaw.

'You should never play the hook shot at the MCG on the first morning of a Test match, because there is always a bit of moisture in the wicket,' he later told *The Cricket Monthly*. 'You are never quite sure of the bounce. I broke that unwritten rule. And I broke my jaw.'

But gradually the surface calmed down and down and down. Australia were 3/104 at stumps on the second day, but from there progressed to 9/419, with wicketkeeper Rod Marsh making an unbeaten 110. McCosker was the last wicket to fall, having come in at number ten with no helmet and his jaw wired. He hooked the first bouncer he faced for four and chipped in 25 runs.

Chappell's declaration meant England needed 463 to win. Despite failing to make triple-figures in the first innings, they had a right good stab at it.

At the heart of it all was idiosyncratic number three Derek Randall. At one point in the first innings, Randall had responded to a Dennis Lillee bouncer by literally doffing his cap. In the second innings, he mostly smashed them for four.[6]

---

4   According to historical reports, a sizeable lunch and plenty of beer are thought to have been factors.
5   Bad news for the queen, who was due to attend on day five. (Possibly seeking to take advantage of cheaper ticket prices for that day.)
6   Lillee bouncers, not caps.

One hit him in the head.[7] He gave it[8] a rub and then did a backwards roll to evade the next one.

The Australia players were sufficiently addled by Randall that when he was given out caught behind on 161, Marsh asked for him to be called back, explaining that he hadn't completed the catch before dropping the ball.[9] Randall added another 13 runs before being more definitively dismissed by Kerry O'Keeffe. O'Keeffe and Lillee then shared the last five wickets as England were bowled out for 417.

Australia had won the match by 45 runs. (Older readers, please consult your notes.)

---

7   A Lillee bouncer, not a cap.
8   His head, not Lillee's bouncer.
9   Same old Aussies, always calling England batters back if they feel their wicket has been taken unfairly.

Queen Elizabeth II being given the honour of meeting Derek Randall.

45

ENGLAND SLIP INTO THE NINETIES

AKA G'DAY, BRUCE

Left-arm philosopher Bruce Reid ruminates on the Cartesian dualism of mind and body, vis-a-vis outwitting the batter vs being injured all the bloody time.

In the ninth episode of the second series of the sketch comedy television show *Monty Python's Flying Circus*, the Pythons introduced us to their conception of Australians. More specifically, of the Australians who occupied the Philosophy Department of the University of Woolloomooloo.

These esteemed professors were all dressed in khaki, with cork hats to keep away the flies. They proudly proclaimed their love of drinking beer and shamelessly questioned the sexuality of their newest colleague with epithets typical of the era (some of the dialogue in the sketch has, let us say, aged poorly). Most importantly, they were all named Bruce.

The writer of the sketch, Eric Idle, explained this lack of nomenclatural diversity as being a reflection of his Australian friends of the time, who, he said, always seemed to be called Bruce.

Yet despite Idle's observation of the prevalence of Bruces, Australia have had a mere handful in their ranks of Test cricketers: Bruce Dooland (who played three Tests in the 1940s), Bruce Francis (three Tests in 1972), Bruce Yardley (33 Tests from 1978 to 1983), Bruce Laird (21 Tests from 1979 to 1982) and, towering above them all, both in height and in cricketing ability, Bruce Reid.

By 'cricketing ability', we don't, however, mean 'batting ability'. In the last fifty years, using the usual twenty-innings caveat, Australia has not had a worse batter than Bruce Reid. From the thirty-four times that he made his way to the crease in Tests, he tallied a mere 93 runs, and was dismissed on twenty occasions. His Test batting average was therefore a measly 4.65, the lowest of the last half-century. In ODIs, his record was even worse: he averaged just 3.76.[1] He doesn't have a T20I batting average, but if he did, you know it'd be dreadful. Bruce Reid's batting was so thoroughly inept that the Pythons themselves would have hesitated to write it into a sketch for fear it was too implausibly absurd.

To the selectors' eternal credit, Reid was never once selected in the Australian side for his batting. He was a bowler. A left-arm fast bowler to be precise, and potentially one of the very best that Australia ever produced.

We can only really talk in potentials for Reid, though, because

---

1 Infamously, he once played out the final over of an ODI against New Zealand without once laying bat on ball to give the Black Caps a stunning one-run victory.

his body was not up to the rigours of Test cricket, and he spent most of his career out injured. (Reid was a skeletal prototype for Ryan Harris, to the extent that the pair finished with identical Test bowling records: 113 wickets from 27 matches.)

When England showed up for the 1990/91 Ashes looking to regain the urn, a few of them might have recalled The Gangliest Bowler Alive, who had somehow played all five Tests against them four years earlier. Tall and painfully thin, Reid took 20 wickets in that 1986/87 series at 26.35. More than handy, yes, but insufficiently threatening to prevent England from comfortably retaining the Ashes.

The following (Reid-less) Ashes series, in 1989, had seen Australia thump England, but we were now in a new decade. The story of the Ashes in the 1990s was unwritten. Sure, we all know now that the author didn't throw in too many plot twists for that decade. But at the time, in those last few years before Shane Warne and Glenn McGrath were invented, the England players must have been hopeful that they might replicate the success of their 1986/87 forefathers. (The 1986/87 and 1990/91 England squads shared four players, Allan Lamb, David Gower, Gladstone Small and Phil DeFreitas, raising a curly question: can you be your own forefather? Let's say you can.)

England lost the first Test of the 1990/91 Ashes by ten wickets, but the result belied the competitiveness of a low-scoring match. Innings scores of 194, 152 and 114 on the first two days on a juicy Gabba pitch were followed by a third day dejuicing, which allowed Mark Taylor and Geoff Marsh to effortlessly run down the 157 needed for victory.

England therefore went into the second Test, at the MCG on Boxing Day, still confident that they could compete with Australia.

Reid would put an end to that idea, taking 13/148 in the match and reducing almost the entirety of the England XI to his personal batting level. Only wicketkeeper Jack Russell and the undismissable number eleven, debutant Phil Tufnell, avoided having their wickets taken by Reid. (Between this effort and The Cat's previously discussed evasion of being part of a Shane Warne Test hat-trick, you might conclude that Tufnell was an underrated tail-ender. This was – and we can't stress this strongly enough – very much not the case.)

Like some kind of non-Euclidean torturer, Reid terrorised the England batters with his unfathomable angle.

Bowling left-arm over the wicket, he repeatedly found the outside edge, sending the ball flying into an understandably alert slips cordon.

In the first innings, four of Reid's six wickets flew to either Ian Healy or second slip Taylor. The exceptions were centurion David Gower, caught and bowled in a display of quite startling athleticism, and noughturion Mike Atherton, caught by Boon at bat-pad.

Despite Reid's six-for, England made 352 and took a 46-run first-innings lead. When they reached 4/147 in their second innings at tea on the fourth day, a 193-run lead, they were in control of the Test.

However, after the break, Allan Border again tossed the ball to Reid, who immediately called upon his cack-handed angular deception to entice an edge to gully from Alec Stewart. This triggered a collapse of 6/3, with Reid finishing with 7/51 from his 22 overs.

Of the seven wickets Reid took in the second innings, six were held by the slips cordon. (The seventh was a very pre-DRS LBW decision against DeFreitas. Umpire Peter McConnell perhaps came across as less impartial than was ideal in this Test. According to Tufnell, on the final day McConnell responded to an enquiry as to the number of balls remaining in the over with, 'Count 'em yourself, you Pommie [expletive deleted[2]]!')

The blitzkReid left Australia needing 197 to take a 2–0 lead in the series, a feat they accomplished just two wickets down. The Test was gone. The series would soon follow. England were toast. The 1990s had begun.

ACTIVITY CORNER

Write a screenplay for a *Back to the Future*–style movie in which four England cricketers go back in time four years to warn their younger counterparts what the Ashes will be like in the 1990s.

---

[2] 'Bastard'.

44

PETER TAYLOR MAKES HIS DEBUT

AKA THE WHO'S 'WHO?'
OF ASHES CRICKET

FUN FACT: Undeterred by the fact people would inevitably assume they'd confused Mark and Peter Taylor, the Australian cricket selectors reportedly also considered calling up Queen drummer, Roger Taylor, for the 1987 SCG Test.

There are cricketers who force their way into the national side through sheer weight of performances at first-class level. Such players amass runs or wickets (or both) in the Sheffield Shield and/or county cricket until eventually selectors are left with no choice but to throw up their hands in statistical acquiescence and usher them into the top tier.

Others, however, do not.

For example, Peter Taylor for the final match of the 1986/87 Ashes. The series was already decided by that point, England's Boxing Day Test win giving them an unassailable 2–0 lead. With the urn gone, the Australian selectors made three changes to the side that had suffered an innings defeat. (Tests after the series result has been determined are when selectors get an opportunity to party.) Out went David Boon, Greg Matthews and Craig McDermott. In came Greg Ritchie, Dirk Wellham and Peter Taylor.

It was the last name that raised eyebrows. 'Peter Who?' read the infamous newspaper headline, and for once the lamestream media got it right. Not a single cricket fan in Australia had a clue who this dude was. 'You mean *Mark* Taylor, right?' was the most common response. 'The opener? Because you've selected a team with only one specialist opening batter.'

'Uh, *no*,' replied the selectors with unconvincing adamance. 'We definitely meant Peter Taylor, the thirty-year-old offie from Sydney's Northern District club, who has only played six first-class matches because he can barely crack the New South Wales first XI.' Then, after a brief pause, 'Let "Fat Cat" Ritchie open.'[1]

Despite the sceptical side-eye from the greater Australian cricket public, Taylor justified his inclusion in the side. He took 6/78 in England's first innings and scored 42 in a 98-run eighth-wicket partnership with Steve Waugh in Australia's second to set up a win, which was secured with just one scheduled over remaining. That was when fellow spinning Peter, Peter Sleep, snuck a ball through John Emburey's defences.

Taylor was named Player of the Match and never played another Ashes Test. He did, however, play a further twelve Tests against other nations,

---

1   Greg Ritchie was nicknamed 'Fat Cat' after the rotund anthropomorphic feline host of the popular children's television show *Fat Cat and Friends*. Did he resemble this costumed character? Let's just say, he didn't *not* resemble him.

along with eighty-three ODIs. This later success at international level does somewhat undercut the absurdity of his initial selection, and leaves open the possibility that there has been a more ridiculous one-Ashes-Test wonder from the past fifty years.

Here are some candidates:

GRAHAM MANOU

When Brad Haddin injured his finger between the toss and the start of play of the third Test of the 2009 Ashes, reserve keeper Manou got a last-minute call-up to the side. He took three catches, and scored 8 and 13 not out in a rainy draw.

Ridiculousness level:

LOW-MEDIUM

Manou was in the squad as a reserve keeper. Any injury to Haddin would have given him a start. Some minor nonsense points for the injury coming after the toss, but that's all.

SCOTT BORTHWICK

The bizarre climax to the even more bizarre 2013/14 Ashes drubbing saw England 'call forth the Borth', as nobody said at the time. Borthwick was summoned from Sydney grade cricket, where he had played one match alongside Brad Haddin. He took three wickets and scored 1 and 4 as Australia completed their clean sweep.

Ridiculousness level:

MEDIUM-HIGH

Borthwick said Haddin was 'a good fella'. Haddin said Borthwick would be 'monstered'. Borthwick got two of his three wickets with full tosses in Australia's second innings – one of which was Haddin.

MASON CRANE

Another 'screw it, let's try a leggie for the last Test' selection from a doomed England touring side, this time in 2017/18. Crane took 1/198 in Australia's only innings, Usman Khawaja stumped for 171. Crane also made 4 and 2 with the bat, succumbing to a Mitch Marsh run-out in the first innings.

Ridiculousness level:

HIGH

The numbers (and run-out) speak for themselves, but this one is also a triumph for wordplay fans. A man named after a machine designed to move rocks for stonecutters? Playing in the same Test as Mark Stoneman? Delicious.

MICHAEL BEER

One of the many intermediary spinners Australia trialled between Shane Warne and Nathan Lyon, and the one specifically endorsed by Warne himself (although not, as far as we can tell, ever endorsed by Lyon, presumably to avoid lawsuits from the Lion Nathan beer-brewing company). Beer took 1/112 in the Sydney Test of the 2010/11 Ashes, and scored 2 not out and 2.

Ridiculousness level:

LOW

The name's a little silly, and Warne's random enthusiasm for him was fun (it's possible that the often-thirsty Warne thought he was made of actual beer). But otherwise a tad dull. Also, Beer played a second Test, a year later, against the West Indies, always a disappointing transgression for one-Test wonder connoisseurs.

JAMES FAULKNER

Faulkner had a great white-ball career, including a Player of the Match effort in the 2015 ODI World Cup Final. His lone Test came at the end of the 2013 Ashes. He took six wickets in that Test, along with two good declaration batting innings of 23 and 22.

Ridiculousness level:

LOW

Faulkner performed well in his sole Test. A perfectly sensible, albeit inexplicably brief Test career, comfortably outshone in nonsense levels by the other one-Test wonder from that Test. (It's arguably quite ridiculous that a cricketer would play one Test, take six wickets, average 16.33 with the ball and never play again – but that's ridiculousness from the selectors, not from Faulkner.)

SIMON KERRIGAN

In contrast to fellow debutant Faulkner, Kerrigan completely forgot how to bowl in his sole Test, sending down a series of full tosses and long hops that Shane Watson brutalised to and over the boundary. Kerrigan's first two overs cost 28 runs. Overall, he conceded 53 runs in eight overs and didn't get to bowl in the second innings. On the plus side, he made 1 not out in his only Test innings. Never took a wicket in international cricket, but was never dismissed either.

PETER TAYLOR MAKES HIS DEBUT

Ridiculousness level:

VERY HIGH

The man took 0/53 from eight overs. Commentators at the time took great pains to assure fans he was 'a much better bowler than we've seen in this Test so far'. Which was pleasing to hear, because imagine if he wasn't?

ACTIVITY CORNER

There are, of course, other one-Ashes-Test wonders from the past fifty years. To choose just four further names, more or less at random: Doug Bollinger (the more sophisticated precursor of Michael Beer), Boyd Rankin, Jonathan Agnew and Chris Silverwood.

Can you make an XI out of the names mentioned in this piece? (Yes, it's tricky, given that most of them are bowlers. But that wouldn't have stopped the selection panel that chose Peter Taylor. You shouldn't let it stop you.)

43

THE LONGEST DAY IN THE HISTORY OF TEST CRICKET

AKA MULLALLY'S BATTING THE DIFFERENCE

England players celebrate finally reaching the end of the longest session in Test history.

England's wheels rarely seem firmly attached for away Ashes tours, and during the 1990s in particular it wasn't really a question of if they'd come off, but when.

On the 1998/99 tour, they came off between the third and fourth Tests.

The first had been drawn, but the second and third were lost by sizeable margins. England then played a tour game against an Australian XI.

It started well enough. Captain Alec Stewart and vice-captain Nasser Hussain both took the game off, but stand-in skipper Mike Atherton made a double-hundred in England's first innings. Graeme Hick made a hundred too.

The batters' cause was helped by Paul Reiffel succumbing to injury after just nine balls. When Michael Kasprowicz also went down later in the innings, Australia A were down to just one seamer, Brendon Julian. Australia A responded to England's 6/469 with a Greg Blewett–powered 4/293.

England then mixed up their batting order to give other players some time at the crease and set about milking what was left of the Australia A attack. Mark Butcher extracted three figures. The plan, apparently, was to bat on and on and then just have a couple of hours in the field towards the end of the match so the bowlers could stay limber. However, as Stewart later told *The Cricket Monthly*, 'Ath got bored and decided he would declare.'

At this point, England's confidence-building exercise transmogrified into a confidence-shredding exercise, as Blewett and Corey Richards chased down 376 in 55 overs. England managed just one wicket – Matthew Elliott for 8.

The integrity of England's wheels had looked pretty questionable in the second Test, when they'd failed to pass 200, and they'd been audibly rattly in the third, when they'd barely scored many more. Now those wheels were off. And it was time for the Boxing Day Test.

England responded to wheel-lessness the way they always did – by mucking about with their team. Alex Tudor was apparently going to come into the side, only to receive from Santa Claus the delightful Christmas gift of a groin injury.[1] England duly

---

1   Not literally. All we're saying is he got injured over Christmas. Although, thinking about it, no one actually said *how* he sustained the injury, so who's to say it wasn't during a bout of Greco-Roman wrestling with Father Christmas?

surveyed their squad and concluded that if a seam bowler was out of action, they could always pick a wicketkeeper instead, and make their previous wicketkeeper open the batting and then move their opener down to three.

These measures both did and didn't work. While a wicketkeeping-gloveless Stewart opened and made a hundred, his opening partner, Atherton, made a duck. So did Butcher, newly installed at three. When number eleven Alan Mullally was dismissed for a rather more predictable duck, England were all out for 270. This seemed handy enough when Australia then fell to 8/252, only for Steve Waugh to forge his way to an unbeaten 122 with the unlikely assistance of Stuart MacGill, who achieved his highest Test score of 43. Australia took a 70-run lead – which immediately looked more sizeable when Atherton secured a pair.

At times like this, weary 1990s England fans were generally content to see a middling, nondescript sort of batting performance. And that's pretty much what they got. Stewart, Hussain and Hick all passed 50 and took England to 9–221, just 151 ahead. At this point, Alan Mullally walked out.

It would be wrong to say that Mullally was the worst batter in the world. It would, however, be fair to say that he moved in those circles. His first-innings duck had been his fifth in his last six innings – surely enough in itself to earn him an invite to a number elevens' cocktail party, where he could discuss the art of missing a straight one with the likes of Phil Tufnell and Bruce Reid.

Despite this, it is an incredible but true fact that Mullally – who finished his Test career with a batting average of 5.52 – thrice batted at number nine for England, and on two of those occasions none of his teammates were unavailable due to broken fingers.[2] The two batters who were considered less competent than him were Ed Giddins, who ultimately secured more Test wickets (12) than runs (10), and – entirely predictably – Tufnell.

A loud and sarcastic roar therefore greeted the single that got Mullally off the mark, tinged with a faint bass note of hopeful desperation from the English contingent in the crowd.

Mullally looked rather nonplussed by the response. Perhaps it pricked something in him, because he swished

---

2   On the third occasion, Nasser Hussain of the Easily Broken Digits had succumbed again.

the next ball he faced, from Stuart MacGill, to the fence for four. A couple of balls later, he repeated the shot for three, which gave him a golden opportunity to be bounced and sledged by Glenn McGrath at the start of the next over – very probably because he'd bounced McGrath out earlier in the match.[3]

Mullally's air hook to that first delivery was followed by an air hoick towards cow corner to the next one. But he wasn't going to let the small matter of completely failing to lay bat on ball prevent him from mime-sledging his adversary. He lifted a hand to shield his eyes from the sun, seeming to suggest that the deliveries were so far from the stumps that he could barely see them, and he then cupped a hand to his ear in anticipation of a verbal response.

Mullally seemed greatly amused by these shenanigans. McGrath didn't. He came round the wicket and bounced the tailender again, who flinch-hooked even more air.

After the next short ball finally made contact with the bat, McGrath went full and straight – only for Mullally to drive him back over his head for four.

The inevitable volley of verbal discontent only brought about another boundary, as Mullally leant back and smeared the final ball of the over to long-on. Eight runs off the over was eight more than anyone had counted on getting from Mullally this innings (or, indeed, any innings).

Not surprisingly, he was out caught and bowled for 16 skying another short one in McGrath's next over, but the 16 runs he had scored would prove crucial. Decisive, even.

Australia needed 175 to win, and at 2/103 it didn't look much of a challenge. However, Mark Ramprakash then took a scorching catch off Mullally to dismiss Justin Langer, and in the ensuing confusion everyone forgot that England were without wheels.

Dean Headley, in particular, rolled in supremely, taking 4/4 in 14 deliveries. That left Australia seven wickets down, but as they were only 14 runs short of victory, Steve Waugh decided to claim the extra half-hour to finish the game.

---

3   'Bounced out' doesn't really do it justice. McGrath fended one directed at his neck, only to get bowled through his legs when the ball backspun upon landing.

This was a peculiarly brutal regulatory option, because an early tea and attempts to make up for a first-day washout meant England had already been in the field for three hours and fifty minutes without a break. Fortunately, they didn't have to play out the full half-hour, because ten minutes later the longest session in the longest day in the history of Test cricket came to a close.

Headley found Matthew Nicholson's edge to take his sixth wicket. Waugh then took a single off the first ball of Darren Gough's next over, which allowed the Yorkshireman to dispatch MacGill and McGrath for ducks.

England had won by 12 runs – four fewer than Alan Mullally had scored.

42

TERRY ALDERMAN'S SECOND-MOST PRODUCTIVE ASHES SERIES

AKA GOWER GLOWERS

Terry Alderman uses his non-bowling hand to signal to the batter how many times he'll take more than 40 wickets in an Ashes series.

Who was most responsible for Australia's 4–0 win in the 1989 Ashes, the series that began the run of Antipodean dominance that continued until 2005?

Steve Waugh maybe? His first Test hundred – 177 not out in the first Test, at Headingley – was immediately followed by his second, when he made 152 not out in the second Test, at Lord's. In fact, it took three Tests and 393 runs for England to dismiss Waugh, and he then came back and made 92 in the fourth Test.

Waugh wasn't Australia's top scorer, though. Not even close. His 506 runs were overshadowed by Mark Taylor's 839 as the fresh-faced young opener made at least a half-century in all six Test matches and generally way more. In the fifth Test, at Trent Bridge, he and opening partner Geoff Marsh batted through the whole of the first day. Taylor finished with 219.

Or what about David Gower? England's new (again) captain invited Australia to bat first in that first Test, whereupon they made 7/601. The only real success for the home team in that innings was wicketkeeper Jack Russell refusing to concede a single bye.

When his team then conceded 528 in the second Test, Gower was subjected to a series of probing questions at the end-of-day press conference. Asked why Neil Foster hadn't bowled from the Nursery End, he emitted an exasperated laugh and replied, 'Right. Thanks, boys. I'm off.' He later said he'd had tickets for the musical *Anything Goes* and a taxi had been waiting for him.

We'll tell you who definitely wasn't responsible for England's debacle, though – chairman of selectors, Ted Dexter. We know this because he said so.

Australia only used twelve players for the whole series, whereas England used twenty-nine. Invited to comment, Dexter said that there was 'nothing to be gained' by looking back. With a level of self-confidence afforded to only the very few, he added: 'I'm not aware of any errors that I have made.'

Maybe Terry Alderman, then. His 41 wickets at 17.36 was a significantly larger haul than England's most successful bowler managed. Neil Foster wouldn't have been able to close the gap much even if he had been given that press-requested spell from the Nursery End, because he only took 12.

Perhaps the craziest thing about Alderman's return is that it wasn't even his weightiest contribution to an Ashes – he'd taken 42 wickets in the 1981 series.

This one didn't require quite

the same workload – just the 269.2 overs, compared to the Herculean 325 he got through in '81. Since England only had to bat once in the rain-affected third Test, that equates to an average of 24 overs an innings. (Not uncoincidentally, that third match was the only one in which he failed to take a five-wicket haul. Fortunately, he was already ahead by that point, having taken two in the first Test.)

The victim with whom Alderman remains most closely associated is, of course, Graham Gooch – although the facts seem a little less remarkable when you dig into them.

It is often reported that Gooch asked to be omitted from the fifth Test so he could work on his game, and it is generally suggested that this was because of his struggles against Alderman. However, while Gooch was indeed out of sorts, he had only been dismissed by his supposed nemesis twice in seven visits to the crease – and he'd made a couple of 60-odds in that time too. Given the volume of overs Alderman was bowling, this doesn't seem too remarkable.

Had the 1981 series influenced perceptions? Alderman had accounted for Gooch a couple of times back then – but again, all that really highlights is the eight occasions when he didn't. (Gooch had missed the sixth Test.)

Maybe the one-day series that preceded the 1989 Ashes helped encourage this view, then? Well, Alderman did get Gooch twice in three matches, but the second time only after he'd made 136.

None of this really seems to add up to much, with hindsight. If anything, the pair's connection only really got inked in after that one-match hiatus, because when Gooch returned for the sixth Test, he was dismissed by Alderman in both innings.

Three of his four dismissals to Alderman during the series were LBW, which had apparently become an area of concern for the batter – to the extent that he is said to have recorded an answerphone message: 'I'm not here right now. I'm probably out ... LBW, to Terry Alderman.'

Is that story just a bit too on-the-nose, and almost certainly untrue? We couldn't hazard an opinion.

Alderman's twin efforts in 1981 and 1989 left him with a bizarre career record. While it's not at all uncommon for a bowler to take roughly half their wickets in one country, it does tend to be their home country, on the basis that this is where they're likely to do half their bowling. Alderman, however, took 83 of his 170 Test wickets in just 12 Tests in England. His average there of 19.33 was markedly better than his average of 34.60 everywhere else.

It makes you wonder what those numbers might have been, had he not missed the 1985 Ashes after committing to an unofficial Australian tour of South Africa in 1985/86 when that country was banned from international cricket because of its policy of apartheid.[1]

That sort of thing represented another 1989 series low point for England, in fact. Midway through the fourth Test, at Old Trafford, it was revealed that sixteen English players had signed up for a rebel tour of South Africa, including nine who'd featured in the series.

This news was preceded by a rather less weighty controversy resulting from footage of Gower (who, by the way, hadn't signed up for the rebel tour) flicking the V-sign behind his back to a heckler in the crowd. With his unmatched aptitude for identifying errors, Dexter immediately phoned Gower to say they had a problem and that he should apologise to the press. Gower said it was not a problem and that he had nothing to apologise for.

All in all, it was a grim summer for the England captain, but he did manage to draw blood from his opposite number at one point. He later told the BBC how he'd invited Allan Border to his house during the Australians' tour game against Leicestershire. There he'd opened a bottle of champagne with an axe[2] and nicked Border's face with a shard of flying glass.

This was, alas, a rare Border nick, the Australian captain scoring 442 runs at 73.66 in the series. But it was not the only axe: Gower received the metaphorical one as captain at the end of the summer.

ACTIVITY CORNER

1. Change your name to 'Ted Dexter'.
2. Immediately become infallible.

---

1   Conversely, it's easy enough to work out what they'd have been had his subsequent ban been longer.
2   He didn't just cleave the fucker. 'Sabrage' is a ceremonial technique where you slide a blade along the seam of a champagne bottle and break the top of the neck away. That said, given all of the above, he could probably have been forgiven for employing a less subtle technique.

41

MITCHELL JOHNSON BOWLS NEITHER TO THE LEFT NOR TO THE RIGHT

AKA HIS BOWLING'S NOT SHITE

Mitchell Johnson shows off his key weapons for the 2013/14 series. From top to bottom: cricket ball, moustache, left arm (obscured).

A six-month stretch between 10 July 2013 and 5 January 2014 saw Australian and English cricketers mine perhaps the richest vein of ridiculousness in the almost 150-year history of the Ashes.

Part of this was due to the fact that in that period the two nations played each other in ten consecutive Tests, across two series, one in each country. The reasoning was that the second series – the one Down Under – should be brought forward by a year so that it didn't take place immediately before the 2015 ODI World Cup, which was also being held in Australia.

'It's always been our aim to break that cycle of two huge events in the same winter,' Steve Elworthy, the ECB's marketing director, told *ESPNcricinfo*.

So it was that England and Australia avoided having to endure a World Cup and Ashes in quick succession until, uh, the very next ODI World Cup, in 2019.

Before we get into any of the actual matches, then, we have the meta-ridiculousness of squeezing ten Ashes Tests into six months for a reason so meaningless that it was undone at the next possible opportunity. Wonderful.

But the fertile absurdity of that six-month period was not just a simple by-product of the number of matches. No, within that vast amount of cricket there was also a disproportionate amount of nonsense per Test match.

We'll get to some of England's antics, particularly in the 2013/14 Ashes, soon. (Like, *incredibly* soon.) For now, though, let's have a look at the ridiculous way that an Australian side, outplayed 3–0 in the 2013 Ashes, suddenly and without warning cohered to match the effort of their infinitely more revered counterparts in 2006/07 by inflicting a 5–0 whitewash.

Of course, when we say 'without warning', we mean 'with a single, very clear, infamous warning' – namely, the warning that Australian captain Michael Clarke gave Jimmy Anderson in the closing moments of the first Test.

With Australia on the brink of a thumping victory, dimpled debutant George Bailey started singing the 'Jimmy, Jimmy, Jimmy' Barmy Army song at short leg as Anderson, England's number eleven, prepared to face up.

Anderson, unimpressed, apparently asked Bailey if he thought he'd ever get a Barmy Army song written about him. (This, in itself, is a beautifully nonsensical retort.)

From there, things escalated. The umpires came in to break it up, while Clarke popped by to inflame matters further. 'Face up, then,' he suggested to

Anderson, before giving the previously mentioned warning. 'Get ready for a broken fucken' arm. Face up.'

The reason Clarke was so emboldened was the terrific form (in both senses of both words) of the freshly moustachioed Mitchell Johnson, the player who, more than any other, defined this utterly mad series.

Johnson, no stranger to Barmy Army songs, had rarely been a source of terror for England batters. Since the second Ashes Test in 2009, his chant-worthy waywardness had tended to undercut any threat his pace might otherwise have offered.

In the first innings of that 2009 Test, with every other bowler conceding roughly three runs per over, Johnson bowled to the left and bowled to the right, turning himself into a meme as he finished with 3/132 from 21.4 overs. Even Anderson was slapping him around by the end of that innings.

Now, four years later, it was time for revenge. Johnson swiftly had Anderson out caught and bowled for 2 to wrap up a first Test win by 381 runs, Australia's first Ashes victory in eight attempts.

Still, everybody knew Johnson was capable of one-off Tests of magnificence. Indeed, that previous Ashes Test win, eight matches earlier, had come courtesy of a Johnson blitz at Perth, Australia's sole bright spot in the 2010/11 series. Consistency was Johnson's challenge, and even he knew it. 'I can have those performances where I can blow a team away,' he would later say. 'And then the next one not turn up.'

In 2013/14, he well and truly turned up for the next one, backing up his Player of the Match performance in the first Test (64, 4/61, 39 not out and 5/42) with an even fierier performance in the second. (In the needlessly Mexican food–influenced words of Shane Warne, Johnson was 'bowling sizzling fajitas with jalapeños on top'.)

On a docile Adelaide pitch, Johnson took 7/40 in England's first innings of 172 all out, and was twice on a hat-trick as he proved too fast and too accurate for ... well, pretty much everybody. In particular, he was far too fast for Anderson, who joined Stuart Broad as a golden duckling (more on *that* dismissal later). Johnson celebrated the Anderson wicket with a bizarre, sideways-scuttling, half-squatting, wordless stare.

The ridiculous form of Johnson would continue throughout Australia's clean sweep. It was not, however, a one-man show. It was an eleven-man show, with Australia remarkably maintaining the same side throughout the entire series. As an indication of how bonkers that was, that XI included Ryan Harris, a man who had spent his career under a leprechaun's curse in which he was gifted immense bowling skill in exchange for surrendering the basic functionality of his knees. Nevertheless, Harris miraculously held it together for five Tests, in which he bowled the ball of the (21st) century (more on that later too) and broke Michael Carberry's bat in two. (Cruelly, there had been no warning from Clarke about the imminent broken fucken' bat.)

The sight of the top and bottom halves of Carberry's broken bat held together only by a sad sticker elicited a niche line of sledging from wicketkeeper Brad Haddin. 'It's a Gray-Nicolls, fellas,' Haddin shouted. 'He's just got stickers on it. It's not a Kookaburra. It's just a Gray-Nicolls.'

If that sounds irritating, you'd be right. For Haddin was at his irritant peak for his opponents throughout the series, albeit usually more with the bat than about one. In the first innings of each Test, Haddin arrived at the crease at 5/100, 5/257, 5/143, 5/112 and 5/97. His scores in response? 94, 118, 55, 65 and 97. Australia's eventual totals? 295, 9/570 (declared), 385, 204

and 326. He finished with the most runs by an Australian wicketkeeper in an Ashes series (take *that*, Adam Gilchrist), driving England fans to despair with his contributions. (In one memorable moment, Michael Vaughan on commentary emitted an audible wail of despair when Haddin successfully overturned what seemed to be the plumbest of LBWs to a Monty Panesar delivery.)

Other major 2013/14 Australian ridiculousness contributors included leg-spinner Steve Smith, who scored two centuries, which brought his tally to three in his last six Ashes Tests. (It was unlikely he could continue that kind of batting form, though, surely.) Smith also did a post-match interview after the fifth Test wearing a baggy green at least three sizes too big for him. A baggy baggy green, if you will.

In contrast, Smith's spinning partner, Nathan Lyon, didn't get a batting average, because he scored 60 runs without being dismissed once.

George Bailey *was* able to be dismissed, out seven times across the series, averaging just 26.14. But such was Australia's improbable dominance that Bailey was carried along for the final few Tests just for the absurd flex of being able to say they stuck with the same team throughout.

Now, that's a rich vein of ridiculousness.

ACTIVITY CORNER

1. Write a song about George Bailey's 100 per cent winning record in Test cricket.
2. Submit it to the Barmy Army.
3. Inform Jimmy Anderson.

40

ENGLAND FALL APART

AKA IT'S ONLY A FLESH WOUND

A perplexed Kevin Pietersen wonders where his bat handle's gone.

Our headline here doesn't narrow things down much, given that apart-falling has historically been one of England's specialties. The 2013/14 tour stands out, however – if only for the jarring contrast between the capable and coherent side that arrived and the brutalised nub of a team that departed with several of its key parts amputated, hacked off or sacked for looking out of a window during team meetings.

England went into the 2013/14 series with much the same side that had not long before been ranked number one in the world. Andrew Strauss and Paul Collingwood were the only significant absences from the squad that had won on the previous Ashes tour in 2010/11. They were replaced by youngsters Joe Root and Ben Stokes, with vague hopes that the two might turn out to be half-decent players in the fullness of time.

As we've covered in the previous entry, England had won the 'home' series 3–0 just a month or so earlier. That meant Australia had lost three Ashes in a row, so as the tour got underway there was cause for English optimism. But then, quite quickly, there was cause for English pessimism.

Preparation for the successful 2010/11 campaign had involved a 'boot camp' in Germany. This time around, the contrived team-building exercise involved doing 'surveillance of terrorists' in Stafford. This largely amounted to following someone around town. 'We were told to blend in with our environments,' remembered the 2.04-metre Boyd Rankin. Even those less physically disadvantaged for the task didn't make much of a fist of it. Graeme Swann remembers Matt Prior trying to surreptitiously order a pint of water in a bar while wearing an England cap and jumper. Everyone thought the whole business was a waste of time. Swann's memory was that they sat in a supermarket car park for fifteen hours a day in a hire car.

When the tour eventually got underway, there were immediately signs that picking pretty much exactly the same group of players as in 2010/11 wasn't necessarily a surefire route to success.

Chris Tremlett, for example, had back surgery in 2012 and hadn't really rediscovered his pace or form. The first warm-up match, against a Western Australia Chairman's XI, was therefore set up as a bit of a bowl-off between him and the other two big seamers, Rankin and Steven Finn. In the first innings, Tremlett managed 0/88, Rankin took 1/92 and Finn took 1/123. Tremlett and Rankin conceded more than four runs an over, while Finn went at over five. Tremlett took another wicket in the second innings and none in the next warm-up match, against Australia A, and on the strength of these performances made the team for the first Test. While his returns weren't dreadful – 1/51 and 3/69 – it proved to be his final international appearance.

The match climaxed with one of Michael Clarke's famously 'funky' declarations when he bravely set England 561 to win. They were bowled out for 179.

The match is widely remembered for the ferocious bowling of Mitchell Johnson and for the fact that England's number three batter, Jonathan Trott, was twice Johnsoned out, having had a torrid time against the same bowler in the one-day series in England that had filled much of the short gap between Ashes series.

The scheduling hadn't really helped Trott here. The final match of Australia's tour of England was on 16 September, and the first match of England's tour of Australia started on 31 October. Discomfited and stressed, Trott spent that period practising.

He went into the nets daily during this period, for hours at a time. 'It was pretty relentless,' he later recalled. Then he went on tour and did extra training in his two days off before the first Test.

It turned out that piling extra pressure on himself did not alleviate the pressure he had been feeling, and the day after the Test was done, he pulled out of the remainder of the tour. With that, England had lost the most reliable number three batter they'd had in years.

Within a month, they'd also lost the most reliable spinner they'd had in years, because ahead of the fourth Test, with the scoreline 3–0 to Australia and the series lost, Graeme Swann retired from international cricket with immediate effect, citing an ongoing elbow injury. His final over had been walloped for 22 runs as Shane Watson carried Australia towards another funky Clarke declaration.[1]

'I did go out with a bang,' Swann observed when announcing his decision. 'That last ball went about 135 metres. I shall forever remember that.'

While there had been sympathy for Trott, Swann's departure was a little

---

1   This was the third time in three Tests Clarke set England a target of over 500 runs to win.

less well received. Former England fast bowler and captain Bob Willis accused him of 'creeping into the lifeboat on the *Titanic* with the women and children'.

Swann was replaced in England's fourth Test team by Monty Panesar, but England also saw fit to drop another 2010/11 luminary, Matt Prior, who had been struggling with his calf (a muscular issue rather than a bovine one). Australia won by eight wickets, so for the fifth Test they dropped another 2010/11 man, Tim Bresnan. He was replaced by Rankin, whose Test debut also proved to be his final outing for England.

Rankin did at least get to play further Test cricket for Ireland, unlike fellow debutant Scott Borthwick, who, as we saw earlier in this countdown, proved to be a less equivocal one-Test wonder.

A third debutant, Gary Ballance, also came into the side, at the expense of Root. Australia won by 281 runs and took the series 5–0.

But the fun wasn't over yet. One key 2010/11 figure, Steven Finn, had somehow managed to avoid appearing in any of the Tests. One game into the subsequent one-day series – having still not played – he was sent home by England's white-ball coach, Ashley Giles. In an extraordinary verdict on his form, Giles explained that Finn was simply 'not selectable at the moment'.

But there's more. Having in some way or other already been denuded of Trott, Tremlett, Swann, Prior, Bresnan and Finn, England surveyed what remained of their 2010/11 squad and thought to themselves, 'Who else can we lose?' They duly decided to sack Kevin Pietersen, who was at the time their leading scorer in international cricket and top scorer in the series just gone.

In its initial, breathtakingly naive statement on the matter, the ECB said only that the management team had concluded it was time to move on, and that they'd be providing no further details. 'No further details' rapidly transformed into a dizzying and endless series of statements, many of which were delayed by legal advice.

Highlights from the ECB included an expression of displeasure that people 'outside cricket' were criticising their decision, as well as a series of leaked documents that outlined various Pietersen crimes. These included taking younger teammates out drinking when they'd been told not to go out drinking, staring out of windows, checking his watch and 'whistling casually' after being dismissed.

Pietersen had of course already been excommunicated once, a year earlier, following a breakdown in relations with teammates and management during a series against South Africa. His supposed 'reintegration' had not perhaps been fully successful. Coach Andy Flower apparently ceased speaking to him for the whole of the fifth Test, and indeed for the whole of the remainder of the tour, after Pietersen allegedly 'ranted' at him following the fourth Test. Pietersen is said to have described captain Alastair Cook as 'weak' and 'tactically inept', before concluding that Flower should 'let the players go out and get pissed'.

In Pietersen's defence, it's hard to see how that plan could have worked out any worse.

39

90S 99S, REPRISE

AKA A CURE FOR THE HICK-UPS

As we shall see when we get to No. 15 in this countdown, being dismissed for 99 makes for a solid foundation of cricketing ridiculousness, particularly if you've got two batters in the same Test (such as Mark Waugh and Mike Atherton) engaging in some comical one-upmanship with their one-shortsmanship. (Flip ahead and read that piece if you like – it's a cracker.)

That moment took place in the 1993 Ashes, and participants in the 1994/95 Ashes must have wondered what they would do for an absurdity encore. After a bit of futzing about with England being generically dreadful in the first couple of Tests (they lost by 184 and 295 runs, respectively – the latter in a Test that inexplicably started on Christmas Eve, and explicably but nonetheless astonishingly concluded with a previously discussed Shane Warne hat-trick), the players returned to the 99 well.

Atherton and Mark Waugh stepped forward again as key participants in the 1994/95 reprise of the double 99 ploy, bursting with admirable ideas for variations on the theme, some of which worked, others of which didn't.

GOOD VARIATIONS

1. Waugh and Atherton chose not to be dismissed themselves, but instead acted as instigators in others falling short of their centuries. This is obviously much stronger material, recasting the pair as mischief-making Road Runners, rather than sad sack Wile E Coyotes.

2. Better still, they chose to not have the 99s be dismissals at all, but instead batters left stranded on 99 not out. Again, great stuff, unlocking the only way in which it's more frustrating to fall short of a century.

BAD VARIATIONS

1. They didn't do it in the same Test this time. Instead, they spread their work out over the third Test (Atherton) and fifth (Waugh). This is just sloppy communication, and self-evidently less comically satisfying.

2. Atherton's one was 98, rather than 99. Come on, Mike, this is basic arithmetic. Do better.

If twins really can read one another's thoughts, Mark Waugh cops a mindful.

Atherton was first up, in his role as captain. England started the third Test in Sydney just as dreadfully as the first two, falling to 3/20 in the first hour. But John Crawley joined Atherton, who revelled in the idea that this was so early in Glenn McGrath's career that he had been selected as 12th man. In the absence of his future tormentor, Atherton made 88. Crawley made 72, and Darren Gough a thumping lower-order 51 as England finished on 309.

Gough then took the ball and tore through the Australians, taking 6/49 to bowl the home side out for 116. England, in the unfamiliar position of being on top in a live 1990s Ashes Test, batted again, looking to set an unchaseable target.

Atherton and his top order Gra(e)umvirate (Gooch, Hick and Thorpe) went to work, moving comfortably to 2/255 forty minutes before tea on the fourth day. That was when Atherton declared, setting Australia 449 runs to win. All very sensible, by-the-book Test cricket.

Except, in declaring when he did, Atherton infamously stranded Graeme Hick on 98 not out.

The Zimbabwe-born Hick had been a county cricket phenomenon, racking up fifty-seven first-class hundreds before making his Test debut, as he waited out the qualification period to play for England. You're always a better player out of the side, and Hick was out of the England side for a looong time. Long enough to make it impossible for him to live up to the hyped-up hopes heaped upon him prior to his Test debut. But to fall as far short as he had – coming into the 1994/95 Ashes, Hick averaged 35.20 from his 29 Tests, with just the two centuries – was disappointing.

All of this added extra bite to Atherton's declaration, a decision that divided England fans at the time and continues to do so to this day. (A prominent critic of the decision? Modern-day Atherton.) On the one hand, Hick knew exactly when Atherton wanted to declare and had dawdled his way towards the milestone. Atherton wanted as much time as possible to bowl Australia out and keep the series alive. The team is more important than the individual and all that. On the other hand, it was two more runs, Michael. How many more overs could it cost? Ten?

Australian fans were much less divided. They unanimously found everything about the declaration hilarious. Especially when Australia held on for the draw anyway.

Solid material from Atherton to

deny Hick so cruelly. Silly, but with a vicious edge, like a clown's cutlass. Pretty much the only thing lacking from the moment, in terms of comedy, was some kind of fraternal relationship between the duo. Oh, and 99 not out would clearly have been better than 98 not out.

Two Tests later, Mark Waugh made neither mistake. England had won the fourth Test by 106 runs, which meant the series could still be drawn with an England victory in the fifth and final Test.

By the time Australia reached 9/402 batting first, however, the chances of England forcing a series-levelling win had faded dramatically. Even more disappointingly, Waugh was about to snatch from Atherton the title of the top-tier ridiculous moment of the series.

Waugh was in the middle as a runner for Australia's number eleven, Craig McDermott. He was at the non-striker's end, while Waugh's brother Steve was up the other end on 99 not out.

In between overs, Steve had urged Mark to make sure he backed up, because 'I'm ready to get my hundred'. Mark, overexcited, took this very literally indeed, racing three-quarters of the way down the pitch after Steve defended the fifth ball of the next Chris Lewis over to his feet. Steve, not as ready for his hundred as previously advertised, remained in his crease as Lewis gathered the ball in his follow-through, spun and lobbed the ball over the retreating Mark's head and into the waiting hands of Gooch, who was moving in from midwicket. Gooch then underarmed the stumps down, with the diving Mark stranded short of the crease, in turn stranding Steve on 99 not out.

Great stuff. Yes, Atherton had intentionality on his side, but on every other measure – being a twin of the ultimate strandee, taking part in a runner-based mix-up run-out, leaving them stuck on an actual 99 not out instead of 98 not out – Waugh had him covered.

Atherton, rightfully devastated, scored just 4 and 8 as Australia won the Test by 329 runs. He was caught by Ian Healy in each innings, as McGrath returned to the starting XI and dismissed him both times. Atherton would succumb to McGrath on a record seventeen future occasions.

One door of cricketing nonsense closes, another one opens.

38

ROOT AND PAINE SUCCESSFULLY OVERTURN DECISIONS... BUT WITH MIXED RESULTS

AKA THE BAIL FAIL AND THE NICK TRICK

Sometimes all you need is a headline to illustrate the eternal and irrepressible ridiculousness of the Ashes. For example, who can forget this timeless classic: 'Joe Root riled by Australia's pre-match handshake plan for Ashes opener'?

What's that? You did forget?

The year was 2019 and the issue at stake was Tim Paine's post-Sandpapergate campaign of malevolent nice guy civility. This was, on the face of it, an ongoing display of humility following the ball-tampering events of Cape Town, which had resulted in the banning of Steve Smith, David Warner and Cameron Bancroft. There was, however, also a feeling in some quarters that there was a certain self-conscious showiness to the whole thing that rang rather hollow.

The centrepiece of Paine's schtick was pre-match handshakes, a goodwill ritual he had introduced at the start of every series. In the bubbling nonsense cauldron that is the build-up to an Ashes series, this had somehow transformed from a perfunctory public-relations act into a knowing, sly act of goading from a load of incorrigible, devious cheats. Not only would Australia stoop to all manner of underhandedness in the series to come, those same hands would also be trying to shake their way to the moral high ground!

This perception is perhaps what fuelled the 'riling' of England captain Joe Root (according to that *Guardian* headline) after he and coach Trevor Bayliss belatedly discovered that handshakes had been listed among the pre-match formalities for the first Test, 'despite not being consulted'.

Much excitement ensued about whether or not Root would reluctantly comply and shake Paine's hand. In the end, he did, because, you know ... it was only a handshake.

With hands maliciously/reluctantly shaken, it was high time for Root and Paine to engage in some proper cricketing nonsense. They duly delivered via a pair of confusing reviews while batting.

First up was Root, who was given not out because he'd been bowled.

On the second morning of that first Test, Root was given out caught behind to James Pattinson. He immediately reviewed the decision, and replays showed the distinct wood-on-ball noise everyone had heard was not in fact bat on ball but ball on stump. Pattinson's 139 kilometres per hour delivery had somehow grazed the off stump without dislodging a bail. Root was therefore somehow not out.

In the immediate aftermath, an astonished Pattinson asked to inspect the bail. After flicking it off the stumps to determine that, yes, it was indeed removable, he hefted it into the air a few times, seemingly questioning its weight.

(Moeen Ali must have missed Pattinson's bail investigation,[1] because later in the innings he confidently unfurled one of the all-time great leaves to a Nathan Lyon delivery that was directed straight at his stumps. There was no ineffectual minor deflection here. This time the off bail tumbled to the earth after the stump beneath it had been knocked clean out of the ground.)

As Australia's wicketkeeper, it was Paine who caught the ball that deflected off Root's stump. The resultant third umpire shenanigans apparently inspired him to undertake his own bizarre review later in the series. No, not the Headingley one. (Don't worry, we'll get to that too.)

Facing his second ball in Australia's second innings of the third Test at Headingley, Paine was rapped on the pad by a delivery from Stuart Broad. Quite understandably, Paine didn't want to be out LBW, so he reviewed the decision and his wish was duly granted. Not only was the ball shown to be going over the top of the stumps, Paine had also edged it before it hit his leg. So it definitely wasn't LBW. Unfortunately for Paine, the ball had then continued on its journey to Joe Denly at gully without ever once making contact with *terra firma*. He was out caught.

This was an uncharacteristically bit-part contribution from the bowler, a man more habitually centre stage whenever ridiculous cricket was afoot. Broad was, however, to make up for it during the fourth Test of the series, on a day when a gale-force wind repeatedly made a show of itself at Old Trafford.

The breeze was sufficiently strong and disruptive that at one point a beach ball blew across the ground at quite a rate of knots. When it reached the middle, Steve Smith triggered a million hackneyed 'seeing it like a beach ball' gags by helping it on its way for four – cue a huge crowd roar as it made contact with the boundary Toblerone.

It was during this period that Broad had to stop his run-up because some kind of empty packet blew across the

---

1   It wasn't just the bail Pattinson was unhappy with. He later expressed his displeasure with the ball by hitting it into someone's pint of beer (and also, in the process, for six).

pitch. Smith pinned it with his bat and handed it to the umpire, but then almost immediately more litter blew across and Broad had to stop a second time.

Already visibly frustrated, a third item of litter then blew towards him. As it fluttered right past his feet, the world looking on, Broad stood and stared at it, the purest and most visceral hatred radiating from every pore. If that item of litter had so much as brushed his toe, there is no doubt whatsoever that he would have had a full Michael-Douglas-in-*Falling-Down* breakdown and immediately sourced a sawn-off shotgun to blow it to smithereens. (Perhaps the 12th man would have run on with a small arsenal from which to choose.)

The most important effect of the wind was that it kept blowing the bails off. The usual recourse in this situation is to deploy the 'heavy bails' – but alas, even these were no match for the phenomenal bluster. The umpires therefore hit upon a straightforward but somewhat jarring solution. They decided that they would simply play the Test match with no bails.

Bails are, you would think, a pretty key piece of equipment for an international cricket match, what with several modes of dismissal being defined by their removal (or otherwise). But no, apparently not. Apparently, you can just play without them.

James Pattinson sat this game out, so his thoughts on the possible ramifications of their absence are sadly not known.

ACTIVITY CORNER

See if you can earn yourself a national newspaper headline by announcing in advance your intention to greet a person or persons in an entirely conventional manner.

An unsuspecting Joe Root falls victim to Tim Paine's devious pre-match handshake plan.

37

ENGLAND REFUSE TO TAKE WICKETS

AKA WAUGH STARS

Trent Bridge scoreboard operators enjoying greatly reduced responsibilities.

One of the key elements to winning Test matches is taking wickets. Indeed, unless you've got a declaraholic opposing captain (and a big hello to Michael Clarke if he's reading!), the only way you can win a Test match is by taking twenty of them.

With this in mind, one of the odder tactical choices of the last fifty years of Ashes cricket was when, in 1989, England chose not to take a single Australian wicket.

Now, this is obviously an exaggeration for half-hearted comical purposes. England did take some wickets during the 1989 Ashes. But of the 120 available across six Tests, the final tally for the England attack was a mere 67 (11.2 wickets per Test), not a colossal return given that, as we've already covered, Terry Alderman alone took 41 for the opposition. The most England took in any single Test was 14, which is not enough to win a match, other than in the most extraordinary of circumstances (more on Mark Butcher later).

England's inability to take Australian wickets might have been forgiven, or at least understood, if they were up against one of the all-conquering Australian teams. Steve Waugh's 2001 team, which gave up 10.6 wickets per Test, is the only Ashes side of the past half-century to prove harder to dismiss than Allan Border's 1989 line-up. (England's 2010/11 tourists, with their three innings victories, are third on the list, losing just 11.6 wickets per Test.)

The 1989 Australian side, however, was not widely thought of as 'all-conquering'. Especially when they first arrived on English shores. Sure, they'd recently won an ODI World Cup, defeating Mike Gatting's England side in the 1987 final. Nobody in Australia had actually seen that happen, though, with the tournament having the geographical, temporal and technological drawbacks of taking place in India before the advent of pay television. For all anybody knew, the whole thing was Australian Cricket Board propaganda.

What Australian fans *had* seen was the 1986/87 Ashes, when Mike Gatting's team retained the urn with a 2–1 series win, as part of Australia's ongoing Decade of Being Shithouse at Cricket™. England also won the annual ODI tri-series on that tour, as well as something called the Perth Challenge, a four-team ODI series to celebrate, uh, the America's Cup yacht race. The 1980s were wild, man.

The point is, England had Australia's measure, alleged World

Cup results notwithstanding, and nobody had any reason to expect that to change. As per the tradition of the time, the England press decreed the Australian side to be 'possibly one of the worst sides to ever tour England'[1] and the 1989 series got underway.

Steve Waugh was the first Australian that England had no interest in dismissing. And this wasn't even the grizzled, hardnosed, take-no-fucken'-prisoners Waugh who would spend the next fourteen years taking obscene delight in crushing England cricket teams beneath his grizzled, hardnosed, take-no-fucken'-prisoners boot. (At least, we assume he took obscene delight in it because of how often he did it. Steve Waugh being Steve Waugh, there was no actual, outward evidence of joy in his merciless demolition.)

This was Steve Waugh 0.9b, a not-quite-ready-for-production release. A dashing bits and pieces all-rounder whose primary bit was piecing together just enough wickets to retain his spot in the side when his batting underwhelmed. (His secondary piece? Doing a little bit of run-scoring, just enough to retain his spot when his bowling underwhelmed.)

Heading into the 1989 Ashes, Waugh had played 26 Tests across three and a half years for a batting average of 30.52 (zero centuries) and a bowling average of 39.32 (two five-wicket hauls). The kid might have potential, but he was taking his sweet time in fulfilling it.

In the first Test, at Headingley, Waugh arrived at the crease at 4/273, after Mark Taylor was LBW to Neil Foster for 136 – his first Test century. Waugh immediately upstaged Taylor, scoring a first Test century of his own, a stylish, helmetless 177 not out, putting on century partnerships with both Dean Jones (79) and Merv Hughes (71!) to guide Australia to 7/601 (declared).

In reply, England made 430 before the tourists added a further 3/230 in their second innings, declaring an hour into the final day. As a sign of the limited expectations that even the players held at the time, Ian Healy later wrote that Australia were 'cock-a-hoop' at lunch, simply because they knew they couldn't lose.

It turned out England could lose, though. And, somehow, despite wickets only falling every 60-odd runs to that point in the Test, the Australian attack

---

1 'They don't even have Shane Warne yet,' sniffed one time-travelling journalist.

suddenly bowled out England for 191 in 55.2 overs to take a 1–0 series lead.

If Australia had shown in that fourth innings the upsides of taking wickets for as few runs as possible, the home side paid little heed. Lord's was next, and Waugh replicated his first Test effort. After England were bowled out for 286, Waugh hit 152 not out to help Australia to 528. This time, his comedy lower-order partner was Geoff Lawson, who scored 74 (74!) in a rollicking 130-run ninth-wicket partnership. Would England finally come around to the idea of dismissing Waugh in the second innings? They would not, and he and David Boon saw Australia to the victory target of 118 for the loss of four wickets (a surprisingly large number in this context).

England very much knuckled down in the rain-affected drawn third Test, though. Their efforts were even rewarded with Waugh's wicket, bowled by Angus Fraser for 43 in Australia's first innings of 424. The dismissal gave Waugh an average for the series. An average of 393.

Waugh carelessly lost his wicket for a second time in the fourth Test, in Manchester, making a massively sub-average 92 as Australia regained the Ashes with a nine-wicket win.

Any suggestion that England might have been getting the hang of this 'dismissing the opposition batters' thing was swiftly quashed, however. Because on a sunny first day of the fifth Test, in Nottingham, Taylor and opening partner Geoff Marsh became the first pair to bat through a full day's play in a Test match in England.

At stumps, Australia were 0/301. Fans back in Australia had spent the entire series waking up to increasingly ridiculous and hilarious scorecards. This was the most ridicularious of the lot. A day of futility for England that neatly presaged the next sixteen years.

Marsh was eventually dismissed for 138 early on day two. The partnership of 329 for the first wicket is still the record for openers in Ashes cricket. Taylor was out for 219 with the score at 2/430. Australia batted into the third day, reaching 6/602 before Border finally declared. England then made 255 and 167 (following on) to lose by an innings and 180 runs.

On the plus side for England, Waugh made an eight-ball duck. So, swings and roundabouts.

36
ENGLAND'S CUNNING PLAN

AKA I LOVE IT WHEN AN ALL-FAST-MEDIUM ATTACK COMES TOGETHER

England's master plan comes together as James 'Faceman' Anderson and 'Howling Mad' Stuart Broad join forces in the fourth Test, with the visitors trailing a mere 0–3 in the series.

In 2021 England arrived in Australia with plans in place. Oh so many plans. Their planning had in fact been so narrowly focused and all-consuming that at times it had seemed as if captain Joe Root and head coach Chris Silverwood had been setting aside time for planning to plan.

The moment that seemed to sum up this monomania had come a few months earlier, at the start of the British summer, when Silverwood had said: 'Playing the top two teams in the world, in New Zealand and India, is perfect preparation for us as we continue to improve and progress towards an Ashes series in Australia at the back end of the year.'

England's Test cricket is often shaped by an Ashes tour – the lead-up as well as the typically explosive aftermath – but relegating Test series against what were, at the time, the two strongest nations to quasi-warm-up status suggested a certain loss of perspective. The comment would perhaps have been forgotten had England made the most of all that 'preparation' and started the series strongly.[1]

What is the start of an Ashes? Is the first ball of the first match the start? (Rory Burns bowled for 0.) Is the first session the start? (England 4/59.) The first innings? (England 147 all out.) The first day? (England 147 all out.) Maybe the whole of the first Test match is the start? (Australia won by nine wickets.) However you sliced and diced it, it didn't feel like England got off to a particularly good start.

Everything hung off that first ball when Rory Burns thumbed his nose at physics and somehow got bowled behind his legs by left-armer Mitchell Starc while seemingly standing in front of his stumps.

For England fans, it was a moment that screamed, 'Don't get your hopes up!' in a shrill, unignorable voice. For Australian fans, many of whom were still under strict lockdown restrictions at the time, awaiting the full rollout of the Covid-19 vaccines, the comedy of England imploding in this manner was a welcome sign that life might be about to return to normal.

To give some sense of how bad a start it was, it was actually quite hard to find an online highlights package

---

[1] England lost the New Zealand series 1–0 and were 2–1 down to India when the fifth and final Test was rescheduled for the 2022 summer in response to a string of Covid-19 positives.

where the superimposed 'play, pause, fast-forward, rewind' controls had auto-faded before Burns's stumps were messed up. As an opening batter, you should really aspire to outlast the video player controls overlay.

Australia clearly felt it had been a long spell of play, though, because upon the fall of that wicket, the subs immediately rushed drinks out with a tremendous sense of urgency. This was quite something, when you consider that, at this point in the match, Starc was the only player on either side to have actually made contact with the ball.

At least five parched Aussies took the opportunity for liquid refreshment. (Starc was not among them.) Maybe they were right. Maybe Burns had been vulnerable due to chronic dehydration.

Impressively, many felt that England's bad start was already well underway even before Starc released that first delivery. Because after all those months – if not years – of planning, the management team had hit upon the idea of not picking their top two all-time leading wicket-takers for the first Test. This was despite both being fully fit and having been the tourists' most successful bowlers on the previous tour.

'It's just precautionary,' said wicketkeeper Jos Buttler, when explaining James Anderson's omission. 'It's obviously a very long series and we want a guy like that to be available to play as much of a part as possible.'

You know what they say: you can't play a big part if you, um … play.

The (over)thinking was that neither Anderson nor Stuart Broad was likely to get through all five Tests, but both were expected to play a major part in the second Test, at Adelaide, which was due to be played under lights. So that was the plan: England began the first Test with one eye (or perhaps four – two each, Anderson and Broad) on the second Test.

Root and Silverwood's England already had a bit of history with day-night Tests. Earlier in the year, they'd pinpointed a Test in Ahmedabad as a golden opportunity to get an edge over India on the basis that the pink ball would assist their fast-medium swing bowlers. They duly went into the match with four seamers and one spinner – only for 28 of the 30 wickets that fell to be claimed by spin. The match was over before the end of the second day – the shortest completed Test match in terms of balls bowled since January 1935.

That was Ahmedabad, though. Adelaide was in Australia. And if there's one thing England's endless planning had extensively covered, it was the types of bowlers needed to triumph in Australia. You need fast bowlers Down Under, and wrist spinners. Everyone knew that fast-medium never worked.

So it was that England replaced their fastest bowler and spinner with Anderson and Broad, resulting in a bowling attack comprising five right-arm fast-medium bowlers. Was this the plan they'd supposedly been honing all this time?

There was, in fact, a nugget of logic underpinning this homogenous line-up. ('Nugget' might be too generous. A flake of logic? A particle of logic dust?) The previous pink-ball Test in Adelaide had seen right-arm seamers have a modicum of success – except Australia hadn't needed five of them. A year earlier, once Mitchell Starc had been whipped out of the attack with the lamentable figures of 0/7 off six overs, no further bowling changes had been required: Pat Cummins and Josh Hazlewood proceeded to bowl India out for 36.

England couldn't even bowl Mitchell Starc out for 36. He made 39 not out. They did, however, manage to restrict the number ten, Michael Neser, to 35, so that was something.

Batting first, the home team made their way to 9/473 and ultimately won the match by 275 runs. Five of the 18 wickets taken by the hapless tourists fell to Root's part-time finger spin and Dawid Malan's occasional wrist spin (which was reserved for desperate occasions, not special ones). Perhaps they should have picked a sixth right-arm fast-medium bowler.

Credit where it's due for commitment to a bit, though. The next time they took to the field for a day-night Test match, in Hobart for the fifth Test, they again did so without a spinner. And this time they only lost by 176 runs.

In a further mark of progress, no England batter made a fifty in that match, so really the bowling was the least of their problems. Burns wasn't bowled first ball either – he was run out for nought having already faced and survived multiple deliveries. A veritable triumph!

Nevertheless, that defeat meant the final scoreline read 4–0. To misquote Scottish poet Robert 'Rabbie' Burns (no relation to Rory), England's best-laid plans had ganged predictably agley.

ACTIVITY CORNER

1. Invite Joe Root and Chris Silverwood round to watch a few old episodes of *The A-Team*.

2. Explain to the two men what it means for a plan to 'come together'.

3. Encourage them to imagine what emotions they might feel were this to ever happen.

35

MARK TAYLOR REFUSES A GIFT

AKA CRICKET, DON'T TALK TO ME ABOUT CRICKET

One of the key plot points in the radio, television, book and towel versions of Douglas Adams's *The Hitchhiker's Guide to the Galaxy* concerns Golgafrinchan Ark Fleet Ship B, a giant spaceship containing the most useless people from the planet Golgafrincham, whom the rest of the population tricked into leaving.

The person in charge of that space ark – a man known only as The Captain – was an affable yet clueless leader who inspired no confidence in his abilities and spent all his time in a tub with his rubber ducky. Australian captain Mark Taylor's nickname of 'Tubby' was not based on this bath-ridden comic character[1] but, heading into the 1997 Ashes, it might as well have been.

Clueless? For sure. In the twelve months prior to the series, Taylor had played nine Tests, scoring 297 runs from sixteen innings at an average of 18.56, with a highest score of 43.

Inspiring no confidence in his abilities? Yep.

The selectors' response to Taylor's dreadful run of form had been to contort the team into increasingly misshapen batting line-ups to cover for his inevitable failure. By the end of the previous Australian summer against the West Indies, Michael Bevan had been added to the batting order as a number seven, doubling as an improbable second spinner. On the South Africa tour that followed, an extra opener was added to cover for Taylor's inevitable early wicket. Matthew Hayden was Taylor's opening partner, Matthew Elliott the number three.

In the presence of ducks? Of course. Although not as many as his recent record might have suggested. Taylor tended to get a start. It was just that the finish popped in soon thereafter.

Despite this, Taylor, like the Golgafrinchan space ark leader for whom he was not nicknamed, remained affable, cheerily making incorrect proclamations to the press or anybody else who would listen that a decent score was 'just around the corner'. *The Hitchhiker's Guide* reminds us 'Don't Panic!', and nobody was don't-panicking better than Taylor.

Taylor's affability was tested, however, on the third day of the tour match against Gloucestershire. When he arrived at the ground, fresh off one

---

1   It was based on him being slightly overweight.

Mark Taylor successfully defends his off and leg stumps.

of those rarer-than-you-might-have-expected ducks in the first innings, a *Daily Mirror* journalist approached and tried to give him a metre-wide bat with a logo reading 'Duckbats Inc'.

Taylor brushed past the giant bat and instead made a painstaking 30 from 106 balls with his normal-sized bat, while new opening partner Elliott (Hayden had not made the Ashes touring squad, having somehow underperformed Taylor in South Africa) and number three Justin Langer both amassed centuries. A couple of promoted bowlers (Shane Warne and Jason Gillespie) then scored 0 and 7 respectively, in a show of poor batting solidarity with their struggling captain.

Because, ridiculously, Taylor, despite batting so dreadfully that the English tabloids were taunting him with oversized props, was somehow still captain of the Australian cricket team. (This is even more ridiculous in retrospect, given that the main reason for the retention of Taylor was the deep concern over the perils associated with letting a Test side be captained by, uh, Steve Waugh. Waugh would go on to claim the best captaincy winning percentage in the history of the game – with the usual 'let's not include outliers from a way-too-small sample size' caveats – while Taylor's captaincy record over his previous *annus ineptitudis* had been five wins and four defeats.)

With nobody willing to tell Taylor he was done, however, he led Australia into the first Test, won the toss, batted first and made 7 (caught Mark Butcher, bowled Devon Malcolm) as Australia collapsed to 7/48, and ultimately 118 all out. And that, surely, was that for Taylor as an international cricketer.

Except no, it wasn't. Because in the second innings, that long prophesied corner around which Taylor had threatened to turn was finally negotiated. He scored 129[2] and saved his career. (Although not the Test, with England winning by nine wickets. More on that shortly.)

With his spot secured, Taylor immediately reverted to his prior shithouse form, averaging 1 with a high score of 2 over the next three Tests.

---

2   Greg Blewett joined Taylor in scoring a first Test second-innings century. The ton was his third in his first three Tests against England, a unique feat. Allowing three centuries in a batter's first three Ashes Tests might be acceptable if the opponent in question was Sir Donald Bradman or Sir Jack Hobbs, but reeked of carelessness from England when the batter was the notoriously unknighted Blewett.

Not that it mattered. The other Australian batters picked up the slack, ton-wise. Elliott scored 112 in the drawn second Test. Noted twin Steve Waugh scored twin centuries (108 and 116) in the third Test to level the series at one apiece. Ricky Ponting returned to the side in the fourth and scored his first (of forty-one!) Test centuries. Elliott also scored 199 in that fourth Test, a fundamentally ridiculous score, before being undone by a Darren Gough yorker, a scorching in-swinging monster of a thing that knocked middle stump out of the ground. It was the kind of ball he probably should have bowled to Elliott before he was pondering his double-hundred celebration, as Australia took a lead in the series that they would not give up.

Mark Taylor, the affable, clueless captain who'd barely bothered to emerge from his metaphorical tub, had led Australia to Ashes victory. England, having blown a 1–0 Ashes lead, thought you all ought to know that they were feeling very depressed.

> **ACTIVITY CORNER**
>
> 1. Design a logo for 'Duckbats Inc.', featuring a hybrid creature that is half-duck, half-bat.
> 2. Present it to a struggling Australian cricketer.
> 3. Ensure that your half-duck, half-bat logo avoids infringing any trademarks of 1990s children's cartoon *Count Duckula*.

34

CAPTAINCY '81

AKA BREARLEY AND MUSE, BOTH, NEWS TO HUGHES

Dennis Lillee sets a new world record for greatest number of sweater removals in a single Test series.

Talk about captaincy in the summer of 1981 and thoughts invariably centre on the dramatic turnaround in Ian Botham's form, which is widely credited as being the greatest feat of personnel management delivered by the man who is often referred to as England's finest captain: Mike Brearley.

A little less scrutinised is the contribution of Brearley's predecessor as captain that summer, Ian Botham. Did England's leader for the first two Tests happen upon and employ some unparalleled means of getting the absolute least out of himself as a cricketer? Perhaps the greatest trick Brearley ever pulled was simply not doing whatever Captain Beefy had been doing.

And lest we forget, there was another captain involved in that series too – Australia's Kim Hughes. Botham's playing performances from the third Test onwards rather overshadow what a wild ride these three captains took fans on that summer.

Botham's heroics aside, arguably the most astonishing development was that Brearley ended up in a position to influence anything at all. Firstly, and most obviously, he was not in the team. Why? Well, chiefly because of a Test record that at that point read 35 Tests, eight fifties, no hundreds and an average of 23.65.

If you want to put that in context, that's a lower average than, say, Vernon Philander, with the same number of fifties (and hundreds). One might argue that averages can be improved – and in many ways the lower they are, the more likely this is – but Brearley was also by this point thirty-nine years old.

So, as a batter, he was past his best, and that best had been worse than Vernon Philander. England duly selected him and asked him to bat at number three.

It is perhaps worth emphasising that allocating him to this key batting slot didn't risk compromising the side quite as much as it ordinarily would have. Three's a crowd, they say, and England had accumulated a crowd entirely composed of them.

In the eight innings leading up to the first Test of the series, Brian Rose, Mike Gatting and Bill Athey had together contributed scores of 10, 5, 2, 0, 2, 1, 3 and 1 in the role. England responded by recalling Bob Woolmer, who had previously been dropped for slow scoring. Woolmer rewarded them with a pair, delivering a nine-ball duck in the first innings, but then picking up the pace in the second innings with a four-ball duck. He then made 21 and 9 in the second Test, so the reasoning presumably ran that England weren't getting runs from number three anyway, so they may as well pick Brearley for his genius captaincy.

Except the very concept of 'Mike Brearley's genius captaincy' was in large part born of what would follow. When he was recalled – Philanderesque batting average and all – he had lost the last three Tests he'd captained against Australia.

However, buoyed by the knowledge that England would apparently do anything to avoid having Geoffrey Boycott as captain, Brearley now led his side with open-minded abandon. The sheer gall of some of his decisions was impressive, to say the least.

After making 10 and 14 in his comeback Test, Brearley concluded that he was now ready to open and so dropped Graham Gooch down to four. This meant David Gower took on the coveted number three spot. Predictably enough, Gower kicked off with a duck before contributing a dizzying volume of runs in the second innings (23).

Brearley made 48 in England's first innings, which turned out to be the highest score of the match. Seeing this and knowing that it was good, he dropped down to five for the fifth Test. This reshuffle also saw Chris Tavaré become England's fourth number three in four matches.

Brearley was dismissed for 2 in the first innings of that Test, and so demoted himself to number six for the second, where he did 50 per cent better by making 3.

In the next match – the sixth and final Test – he was back at number five in the first innings, having apparently promoted himself up the order to protect debutant Paul Parker. Brearley's protection came in the form of a duck. Three balls later, Parker also made a duck.

In the second innings the two men swapped round. Parker's 46-ball 13 perhaps provided sufficient protection that Brearley could come out and make his highest score of the series, 51 runs that actually did an awful lot to secure a draw and a 3–1 series victory.

But lest you think that Brearley's nonsense captaincy was restricted to superpowering Ian Botham and setting the batting order to 'shuffle', it's worth highlighting his most outrageous gambit of all: pretending to Bob Willis that he wasn't bothered about no-balls at Headingley, when England were defending 130 and Willis had bowled 28 of them in an innings in the previous Test. (We'll return to this in a bit more detail later in the book.)

Remarkably – impossibly, you would think – Australian captain Kim Hughes actually went one better in the ridiculousness stakes. In contrast to Brearley, Hughes's idiosyncratic captaincy was generally more apparent in the field – most eye-catchingly when he repeatedly hopped like a frog into Geoffrey Boycott's eyeline while fielding at silly point to spinner Ray Bright.

The central pillar of Hughes's on-field nonsense, however, was his breathtaking reluctance to ever bring on a fifth bowler. Throughout the series, the Australian bowling attack invariably comprised four men, and those were the only four bowlers he was going to use – unless he could get away with using three of them. It wasn't until the second innings of the sixth Test that he finally gave a fifth bowler an over.

But even this doesn't really tell the story, because even within his frontline four (or three), some bowlers shouldered a far heavier workload than others. There was no finer example of this than the first innings of the first Test, where Hughes asked Terry Alderman to bowl 42 per cent of Australia's overs.

Even in a short innings, this is quite a lot to ask of your opening bowler, given that he is only permitted to bowl from one end. Hughes clearly felt Alderman had been underbowled, however, and so never took him off in the second dig. Alderman finished with figures of 5/62 from 19 overs.

Could Hughes be persuaded to risk a part-timer in a longer innings? No, he could not. In the first innings of the second Test, England batted for 124 overs. Australia's spinner, Ray Bright, delivered 15 of them. The remainder were shared between Alderman, Dennis Lillee and Geoff Lawson, who took 7/81 in 43 overs. The same four men bowled all 98 overs in the second innings too.

Over the course of the third Test, Alderman was again entrusted with the donkey work. His 54 overs across the two innings somewhat outweighed those served up by the fourth bowler, Bright, who got through ... four.

By this point, Alderman and Lillee knew where they stood (either at the top of their mark or glassy-eyed at fine-leg). The two men bowled 89 overs in the fourth Test and 151 in the fifth, and still Hughes didn't turn to a fifth bowler.

But then, finally – finally! – as they worked their way through another

105 overs in the sixth Test, Hughes (presumably accidentally) brought Graham Yallop on for eight overs.

You would think that as far as sheer pig-headed refusal to acknowledge reality goes, this would be hard to beat. But no – Hughes outdid even this.

In an interview after the fifth Test of what is widely referred to as 'Botham's Ashes' – the future Lord Beefy having delivered three of the most astonishing performances in Test history in successive Tests – Hughes repeatedly pronounced the first syllable of the great all-rounder's surname as if it rhymed with 'cloth'.

An incredible hundred to turn around a Test match after following-on, a bowling burst of 5/1 to win the next Test, and an astonishingly percussive hundred in the most recent match to secure the Ashes for England – and the Australia captain still doesn't know your name.

33

BETH MOONEY TAKES A CHANCE

**AKA MEG LANNING
TAKES A CHANCE**

Beth Mooney's unbroken jaw, plus several other intact Beth Mooney components.

Meg Lanning was not a captain who enjoyed taking risks. Infamously, during the 2019 Women's Ashes Test, she refused to declare during Australia's second innings.

Australia had already taken a 6–0 lead in the multi-format series by winning all three matches of the ODI leg. As holders of the Ashes, they therefore needed only to draw the Test to retain the urn. When rain washed out most of the second day of a four-day Test, Australia were 5/341 in their first innings. Lanning did not close that innings until shortly before lunch on the third day, declaring with Australia 8/420.

Desperate to win, England got beyond the follow-on mark as quickly as they were able. They declared 145 runs behind, just before lunch on the final day, in the hope that a bold declaration from Lanning might give them a sniff of victory.

The odour-hoarding Lanning was having none of it. *If we don't lose this Test, we don't lose the Ashes*, she reminded herself. And Australia therefore batted out the last two sessions of the match, finishing on 7/230 when stumps were drawn.

The journalists were critical of Lanning. 'That the Test did ultimately finish in a draw … can therefore be placed squarely in the hands of Australia's conservatism,' argued Raf Nicholson in *The Guardian*.

It wasn't just the UK press either. Writing for the ABC, Geoff Lemon suggested that 'Lanning could have declared with about 50 overs to bowl and 250 ahead', before pointing out that 'the Test would have been on a fourth-day pitch with players around the bat, and in the unlikely event that England got close, 10 players could have stood on the fence'.

Lanning didn't seem to care about the criticism, claiming that England didn't deserve to be given a chance to win. 'Next time, take more wickets. Or live in a country that rains less,' seemed to be the gist of her counterargument. And when Australia won the T20 leg of the series 2–1 to secure an Ashes win, complaints about her Test match tactics were mostly forgotten.

But not completely. After the 2019 Ashes, Lanning continued to lean even more heavily into the idea that if you don't lose matches, you tend to win an *awful* lot of trophies and tournaments. Why not, then, simply build the greatest women's cricket team that has ever existed? A team so far ahead of all rivals that the concept of losing a cricket match was more or less off the table? That would eliminate all kinds of risks.

Employing this conservative strategy, Lanning defended the T20 World Cup in 2020, defying sluggish early batting performances, star all-rounder tournament-ending injuries, torrential rain, looming global pandemics and a Katy Perry concert to hold the trophy aloft in front of a packed MCG. She then led Australia to an undefeated defence of the trophy in South Africa in 2023, and on a similarly unbeaten march to a Commonwealth Games gold medal in 2022.

In the ODI format, she reclaimed the ODI World Cup in 2022 by once again reverting to the unimaginative strategy of having her team win every match in the tournament. (Well, not *every* match in the tournament. Just the ones they played.) This 'never lose' idea was one they'd honed in a 26-match, three-year unbeaten streak between 2018 and 2021, and it served them well.

All of which makes what Lanning did in the Test match of the 2021/22 Women's Ashes even more unexpected.

This time, the T20 matches were played first. Two of them were rained out, with Australia winning the one that was played, to take a 2–0 points lead into the Test match.

The Test followed a similar pattern to the one in the previous Ashes. Australia batted first and made 9/337 (declared). In reply, England made 297, with captain Heather Knight scoring 168 not out. But with Australia on 2/12 in their second innings, rain arrived, removing most of the third day's play.

On the fourth day, Beth Mooney and Ellyse Perry led Australia out of that tricky start, before Tahlia McGrath and Ash Gardner batted Australia almost out of reach of England, pushing the lead past 200 with less than half a day's play remaining. So far, so similar to 2019.

And then, suddenly, we weren't in 2019 anymore. Because from nowhere Lanning declared. Perhaps she hadn't been as impervious to the criticisms of the previous Ashes as she'd seemed. Perhaps, after a couple of no-result T20s, she was sick of sharing points with England. Or perhaps she simply wanted to experience the mad, giddy adrenaline rush of maybe, possibly, perchance losing a cricket match.

If it was that last option, then England were happy to oblige. Lanning set a Lemon-approved target of 257 in 48 overs, and England went for it, apparently unaware they were effectively playing an ODI, the format Australia more or less never lost.

England's oblivious top three of Lauren Winfield-Hill, Tammy Beaumont and Heather Knight therefore laid a foundation of 3/166 after 33.1 overs, before Nat Sciver-Brunt and the six-hitting Sophia Dunkley accelerated to reach 3/212 off 38 overs.

With just 45 runs needed off ten overs, a desperate Lanning scattered the field and called for defensive bowling. These updated tactics were rewarded with the wickets of a frustrated Sciver-Brunt and Amy Jones. But with Dunkley, 45 not out from 31 balls, still hitting boundaries, England remained firm favourites. They headed into the last five overs with five wickets in hand and just 25 runs needed for victory.

Lanning's gamble had seemingly backfired. Taking risks? Bleurgh. Who needs it? Whatever happened to good, old-fashioned, risk-free never-losing? That's the way to go about your cricket, surely.

One Australian was still willing to take a risk, however. That mad Australian was Beth Mooney.

Ten days earlier, Mooney had been struck in the face by a wayward cricket ball while receiving throwdowns from coach Matthew Mott. Stunned by the blow, the bloody-mouthed Mooney removed her ineffectual helmet and walked out of the nets, where the medical staff noted, in the way that medical staff sometimes do, that her jaw was swelling 'significantly'.

Mooney was taken straight to hospital, where scans confirmed her jaw had been broken in two places. She underwent immediate surgery, had her mouth wired and was restricted to a liquid diet, but somehow passed a fitness test in order to take part in the Test match.

Given all this, when Dunkley flat-batted Alana King into the deep, it might have been understandable for Mooney, as the nearest fielder, to have hesitated. Instead, she charged around to take a fearless, diving, tumbling catch. It was the exact kind of catch that oral surgeons, as a rule, recommend eliminating from your rehabilitation routine.

Mooney didn't have an awful lot of time to contemplate what might go wrong. The ball might have fallen short of her grasping hands and bounced straight into her face. An awkward landing might have re-smashed her jaw, ruining the whole vibe of this thrilling Test and causing her to miss the imminent World Cup.

Best, then, not to think about it. To just ridiculously go for it.

Mad behaviour from the metal-mouthed Mooney.

But it was mad, match-momentum-modifying behaviour. Because suddenly Australia were all over England. Wickets tumbled and, nine wickets down, the match ended with Kate Cross desperately blocking out King's final over, with Australian fielders all around the bat.

Yes, the match ended in a draw, just as in 2019. But Lanning's declaration and Mooney's madness had resulted in one of the most thrilling conclusions in all Ashes history.

Happy now, journos?

32

STEVE WAUGH HAS A HEADACHE

AKA A GAME OF HOHNS

Steve Waugh trudges off the MCG, knowing that, barring something miraculous in his next Test (e.g. a century off the final ball of the day, passing the 10,000 Test runs milestone and equalling Bradman's record for most hundreds by an Australian – that kind of thing), his career is over.

Steve Waugh had a headache. A migraine, in fact. This was about to become a problem for the Australian captain.

Australia had started the fifth day of the fourth Test of the 2002/03 Ashes on 0/8, needing a further 99 runs to secure victory and take a 4–0 series lead. Easy enough for a side whose previous three victories had been by 384 runs, an innings and 51 runs, and an innings and 48 runs. Yes, a mere ten-wicket victory at the MCG would be a downgrade on those efforts, but there was nothing to be done about that now. Sort it out, Haydos and JL, and we'll try to do better in Sydney.

From the first ball of the day, however, Matthew Hayden skied an Andy Caddick short ball to substitute fielder Alex Tudor. A predictable counterattack from Ricky Ponting was ended by Steve Harmison with the score on 58, and the gangly fast bowler also dismissed Damien Martyn three balls later to just about keep England in the contest. (One of the subtler ridiculous aspects of this final day's play was England using just two bowlers – Harmison and Caddick – after Craig White suffered a side strain and Richard Dawson's spin was deemed unhelpful to the cause.)

As Martyn exited, the be-headached Waugh made his way to the crease to face this fired-up two-man England attack, cheered on by a rowdy Barmy Army.

Australian chairman of selectors Trevor Hohns also had a headache. His was metaphorical. Waugh had been in mostly dreadful batting form for eighteen months. Ever since the previous Ashes in England, in fact, when he'd stubbornly made a century on one leg after an ostensibly miraculous but in fact massively unconvincing 'recovery' from a calf tear.

Between the 2001 and 2002/03 Ashes series, Waugh had played a dozen Tests, scoring just 448 runs at an average of 28.00, with a lone century. His hard-earned 50-plus Test average had returned to 50-minus, dipping to 49.91 heading into the 2002/03 Ashes.

The headache for Hohns was that, despite the slide in form of this proxy Waugh, the Australian team kept winning. Sure, he was willing to remove the captain if the team started losing. He'd done that with the limited-overs side a year earlier, installing Ricky Ponting as the new ODI leader. But dropping Waugh from the Test side while they were winning? That was going to require some truly overwhelming evidence that the skipper was past it.

Fortunately for Hohns, Waugh arrived at the crease on that final day of the Melbourne Test and provided that exact evidence by playing the most absurd innings of his career.

Waugh's scores in the series to date had been 7, 12, 34, 53 and 77, an innumerate Fibonacci-esque steady improvement in form from limited opportunities. His 77 in the first innings had even seen him return to the more flamboyant shot-making of his youth, crashing fifteen boundaries as Australia amassed 6/551 (declared), with Justin Langer scoring 250, Hayden 102 and debutant Martin Love 62 not out.

England replied with 270, with White's 85 not out the only score above fifty, and Waugh enforced the follow-on. (Despite what everybody remembers, Waugh enforced the follow-on every time he had an opportunity to do so after the one that backfired in 2001 courtesy of Rahul Dravid and VVS Laxman. Check the scorecards if you don't believe us.)

In England's second innings, the somewhat addled Michael Vaughan, who had spent most of the series blissfully unaware he was part of a losing team, scored 145. It was his second of three centuries for the series and helped set Australia their 107-run target for victory.

That target had been whittled down to 49 when Waugh and his headache faced up to his first delivery, the final one of a Harmison over. Afterwards, Waugh would explain that the migraine had made him dizzy. But not, alas, the kind of Dizzy who would famously score a double-century against Bangladesh four years later.

This was more the kind of dizzy that saw Waugh get off the mark by inside-edging the next ball he faced over leg stump to the fine-leg boundary, just wide of the diving keeper James Foster.

Later that over, Harmison bowled a replica of the rising short ball that had found Martyn's outside edge. Waugh also got a thick edge and it sailed comfortably through to Foster's gloves. Except, astonishingly, nobody on the England team bothered to appeal, the sound of the edge drowned out by the raucousness of the Barmy Army. (So loud was the crowd that it apparently drowned out the *sight* of the edge as well. Really quite impressive soundwaves.) Sure, Foster gave the umpire a curious glance and Marcus Trescothick raised his arms to the vicinity of his head, but that was the extent of it. Not quite the full-blooded appeal one might expect for the wicket of the Australian captain and a scorer of almost 10,000 Test runs.

Waugh didn't walk, in much the same way as the sun doesn't rise in the west. Upon seeing the replay on the big screen, Foster led a belated appeal, but to no avail. As his captain, Nasser Hussain, clarified after the match, 'You've got to appeal to get people out. You can't just, three hours later, say "Howzat?" or ring them up in their hotel room or something.' (Although imagine if you could! What a sport!)

No matter, because the next ball saw Harmison toss one full and wide outside off stump. Waugh went for his trademark back-foot cover drive but only succeeded in drilling it straight to Hussain diving forward, right and low, to take a smart catch. He hurled the ball skyward in celebration. Waugh trudged off, but his departure was interrupted by Langer calling him back. Umpire David Orchard had signalled a no ball.

'Out' twice in two balls, Waugh faced up again and drilled the next ball straight back past Harmison for four to see out the over. It was the only convincing shot of his innings.

Hussain, as ruthless as Waugh at his best, began giving Langer the single to keep this Waugh-at-his-worst on strike. Eventually, Caddick got him, caught at second slip, bringing to an end a half-hour innings of 3/14 so ridiculously dreadful that it united Australian cricket fandom. Waugh had been a great batter, yes. One of Australia's finest, for sure. But he obviously no longer had it.

Hohns pencilled in a chat with the skipper about calling it quits after the Sydney Test.

Waugh, of course, had other ideas. He took an eraser to Hohns's pencilled-in chat by instead producing an instantly iconic (and ridiculous in its own right) century, completed on the final ball of the second day of the fifth Test, in front of a packed SCG. Waugh's migraine was gone.

Hohns, for his part, put a wheat bag over his eyes until his headache finally went away when Waugh signed off the following summer against India.

31

JAMES VINCE SUCCESSFULLY AVOIDS NICKING ONE FROM MITCHELL STARC

AKA TOUCHED BY AN ANGLE

James Vince is aghast at the startling decline in his nicking powers.

What was the most extraordinary aspect of the extraordinary delivery with which Mitchell Starc bowled James Vince at the WACA in 2017? The big left-armer launched it from around the wicket and wide on the crease, and tracking data calculated the ball would have missed a second set of stumps on the leg side had it not spectacularly redirected towards off stump upon pitching.

However, that jaw-dropping deviation[1] arguably ranks only second for extraordinariness behind the fact that the victim only missed it by a mere 20 centimetres.

James Vince wasn't thought good enough for the England Test team at the start of the 2017 domestic season. However, three 50-plus scores in seventeen County Championship innings saw him (somehow) force his way into the Test side for the Ashes tour that followed.

Reactions to the news among England fans were, shall we say, mixed.

Even without that deafeningly meh case for inclusion, Vince had already established a firm reputation by this point. That reputation hinged on an irrepressible penchant for airy off-side drives. Some of these airy off-side drives sent the ball careering to the fence, persuading all who witnessed them to conclude, 'This boy can really play.' Others were edged behind. The one thing almost everyone agreed on was that the ratio between the former and the latter was not satisfactory for Test cricket.

The first taste of this predilection had come on Vince's Test debut, against Sri Lanka, when he had hit two fours and then edged to slip while trying to hit a third. The rest of that summer followed a similar template – basically a 'worst of David Gower' montage viewed in a mirror. The Gower parallel is especially apposite here because no other batter has better illustrated an eternal rule about batting that most definitely applies here: the more sweetly you can time a cricket ball, the more harshly you will be judged when you do not.

Vince's entire international career had thus far been an exercise in raising opinions so that they might then be more thoroughly and completely dashed. Yet now he was back in the

---

1 'Deviation' seems entirely the wrong word here, given the level of redirection. No one would ever say the ball 'deviated' off the middle of a player's bat, over the grandstand and into the Swan River, would they?

England Test team on the strength of no one else being much good either.

The selectors' theory was that the ball doesn't tend to swing as much Down Under, so Vince would have to find a new way to get out. So it was that with a Test batting average of 19.27 and that so-so county summer under his belt, he arrived in Australia to make the England number three spot his own.

Utterly bizarrely, on day one of the series, it very much felt like that might happen.

As we've already established,[2] England fans know a thing or two about day one at the Gabba, so when Alastair Cook was dismissed in the third over, everyone in the Northern Hemisphere immediately went to bed. Cook was the one man with a fairly decent track record of hanging around at the crease in Australia. Vince was … well, he was James Vince. It was clearly bedtime.

And yet! Maybe there was something in that theory about the lack of swing negating Vince's one glaring weakness, because while the dreamy fours materialised, the nightmarish edges did not. A stand of 125 with Mark Stoneman surpassed any England partnership in the whole of the previous tour.

Vince was playing silky, chanceless cricket, and everyone agreed he definitely wasn't going to edge behind this time. A hundred was a certainty. Or at least it would have been if he hadn't run himself out on 83. (You can always rely on Nathan Lyon to secure a run-out.)

Stung, Vince went back to the two things he knew best over his next four innings: an edge to slip, an edge to the keeper, an edge to slip and an edge to the keeper.

He then started batting reasonably effectively again, and after making 55 runs in England's second innings in Perth, came up with a flawless new method to avoid edging behind. There was, quite simply, no way this new method could fail.

All he had to do to avoid losing his wicket to an airy drive was to persuade a left-arm bowler, operating round the wicket, to aim a 145-kilometre-per-hour delivery 30 centimetres wide of leg stump, only for it to hit some sort

---

2   And you can expect that establishment to be firmed up yet further in future chapters.

of chasm that would redirect it into his off stump.

Because Starc was not just bowling around the wicket when he delivered this jaw-dropping monstrosity. He was bowling around the wicket from the absolute edge of the crease, increasing the angle still further. The distance between where conventional physics dictated the ball should have gone after pitching and where it actually went was phenomenal.

Not to undercut that previous sentence at all, but ball-tracking data calculated that 'phenomenal' distance to be 42 centimetres. If that doesn't sound like much, see if you can move 42 centimetres in, what, a tenth of a nanosecond?

And it's not like Vince knew in advance in which direction he would need to move – or indeed that he would have to do so at all. As the ball was delivered, there was in fact no suggestion that he would be required to make a 42-centimetre, tenth-of-a-nanosecond movement correction while already committed to playing a shot targeting the patch of air where the ball should, by all conventional logic, have ended up.

What Vince needed to do in that less-than-colossal span of time was identify that the ball had unexpectedly skewed in a nonsensical direction, recalibrate his own internal human ball-tracking to calculate the new trajectory, and then redirect various parts of his body to counter this.

Literally impossible – but Vince's reputation was now so firmly established that many England fans nevertheless threw up their hands in dismay. 'Shabby batting!' they cried. 'You're better than that!'

Vince wasn't better than that. It also seems fair to assume that if even James Vince couldn't nick a ball that seamed away, while confidently presenting the full outside edge of his bat, then surely no one could.

It was, if anything, borderline miraculous that Vince only missed the ball by about 20 centimetres. This element in itself cast Vince's whole career in a different light. If a batter could get that close to a ball as ludicrously unplayable as this, he must be touched by genius. While Vince didn't deserve the criticism for missing this one, perhaps he *did* deserve greater opprobrium for only barely clipping all those other ones.

His brain still scrambled, Vince was dismissed LBW in his sole innings in the next Test, in Melbourne, before reverting to his usual combo of being caught by the wicketkeeper and at slip in the final Test.

JAMES VINCE SUCCESSFULLY AVOIDS NICKING ONE FROM MITCHELL STARC

ACTIVITY CORNER

1. Study trigonometry at the highest possible level.

2. Re-examine the angles of the Starc delivery to Vince.

3. Can you reconcile this with the axioms of geometry? If so, how? Show your working.

30

ALLAN BORDER AND JEFF THOMSON FALL SHORT

AKA A SPANNER IN THE WORKS

Allan Border experiences a sudden flashback to the 1981 Ashes as Jeff Thomson wonders who stole his clothes.

When Pat Cummins coolly guided his team to victory by two wickets in the first Test of the 2023 Ashes, wee-hours-punishment gluttons back in Australia could scarcely believe their bleary eyes.

Because, prior to the Australian captain's winning glide to the third man boundary, one of the subtler pieces of Ashes ridiculousness from the past fifty years had been Australia's complete inability to win a tight Test. Despite the purported powers of the baggy green, virtually every match that went into its endgame with the result undecided was eventually resolved in favour of England, rather than those with the advantageously voluminous and hued headwear.

Heading into the 2023 Ashes, for all margins of victory closer than 20 runs or two wickets in the last fifty years, the record stood at seven England victories and none to Australia. Expand it to margins within 50 runs or three wickets, and England's pre-2023 advantage was ten to nil.[1] (Even the Australian women weren't immune to this tendency to lose tight matches. There's been only one Ashes Test between the women in the past fifty years that's finished with a margin within these definitions, in Adelaide in 1984/85. England won it by five runs, as we saw back in No. 47.)

Sure, some of these matches had no impact on the outcome of the series. England's Boxing Day win by 12 runs in 1998/99, for example, eventually saw Australia hold the urn by a 3–1 scoreline instead of 4–0. Similarly, England's win by 19 runs at The Oval in 1997 dragged back a potential 4–1 series result to 3–2. And the 14-run victory in 2013 meant England won the Ashes 3–0 instead of 2–1.

Other tight wins to England, however, turned series. The ultimate result of Ben Stokes's one-wicket win at Headingley in 2019 was a 2–2 series draw rather than a 3–1 Australia win. Flip the result of England's two-run Edgbaston win in the 2005 Ashes and the most important series of the last half-century becomes just another instalment in Australia's long streak of victories.

This curious trend of England holding their nerve in tight Tests in a way that Australia couldn't can, of

---

1   Australia did win the Centenary Test in 1977 by 45 runs, but there was no Ashes at stake. (Yes, despite its inclusion in this book.)

course, be traced back to the absurd escapades of Ian Botham during the 1981 Ashes. In consecutive Tests at Headingley and Edgbaston, Botham conjured miracles that directly led to wins by 18 and 29 runs respectively. (You surely know by now that this stuff is on the way.) Flip either of those improbabilities to the more likely outcome and the series would have been tied. Flip both of them and suddenly it's *Australia* winning the 1981 series 3–1. In this strange, alternative timeline, Botham's legendary status is reduced to plain old common-or-garden greatness. Mike Brearley? More like Mike Nearly. Kim Hughes? Kim Doesn't-Lose.

Still, in our own timeline Botham's idea of performing impossible feats of cricketing heroics to win Ashes Tests is a compelling one. And so, when number eleven Jeff Thomson joined Allan Border with 74 runs needed for victory, late on the fourth day of the MCG Test in the 1982/83 Ashes, the duo decided to give it a crack.

Border had been out of form, with scores of 8, 32 not out, 0, 15, 26 and 2 in the series so far. As a batter, Thomson never quite attained anything that could be described as 'form' in his twelve-year Test career. So far this series, for example, he'd made 5 not out, 3 and 1. There was no way this pair was adding 74 more runs.

Still, recent batting form had no bearing on one's ability to summon startling feats of cricketing magic. Botham – who made a pair in the Test prior to Headingley '81 – had taught them that.

So Border and Thomson went to work. England captain Bob Willis – a known participant in cricketing miracles – spread the field to Border to get Thomson on strike. But the former pinched end-of-over singles and scrambled to turn mid-over ones into twos, while the latter held firm whenever the strike-farming fell fallow. England also contributed to the madcap fun of the final hour, adding a five into the mix via four overthrows.

The seemingly inevitable fourth-day finish to the Test didn't arrive, as Border and Thomson halved the runs required from 74 to 37, heading to stumps on 9/255.

On the fifth day, the MCG threw the gates open. Ten thousand freeloading fans showed up at the start of play. That number would double throughout the morning, as Border and Thomson whittled down the chase.

As the runs required shrank into the low twenties, England again added a slapstick touch to events, with panicky fielders colliding as Border called a dozing Thomson through for a strike-retaining single.

With ten required and Australia closing in on a miracle, Willis went for the counter-miracle, summoning Botham to the bowling crease. True to form, Beefy soon manifested one, finding Thomson's outside edge. The ball flew low and fast to Chris Tavaré at slip, who spilled the chance. Australia took a run to bring the target down to single figures.

A Border cover drive for three, then a leg glance for two saw Australia within four runs of victory. From the final ball of his over, however, Willis bowled a dot ball, which left Thomson on strike for the next.

In Australia, the Channel Nine television coverage then went to the usual end-of-over commercial break. In most regions, this was an advertisement for Sidchrome spanners. By the time viewers returned from this torturous touting of torque-tailored tools, the match had finished.

What fans at the ground had witnessed live, and television-watchers had to wait for the replay to see, was Botham – inevitably Botham, unavoidably Botham, inescapably Botham – once again bestowing upon his team an edge from Thomson. Once again, the ball flew to Tavaré in the slips. And, once again, Tavaré dropped the chance,[2] a far easier catch than the one a few overs before.

But this time there was a crucial difference. This time, Geoff Miller swooped around from first slip to gather the rebound.

Australia had been one shot away from the highest ever tenth-wicket partnership to win a Test match. Instead, England had won by three runs, at the time the closest margin of victory in the history of Test cricket.

Given England's tendency to take home the win in every close match, it's no wonder that Australia would eventually latch onto the idea of never letting the Tests become close, thrashing England by as big a margin as possible at every opportunity between 1989 and 2005. Good tactics. In retrospect, it's weird they ever went away from it.

---

2   Imagine dropping a chance off Botham with the match on the line. Imagine doing it twice!

29

A ZILLION RUNS AT THE GABBA

AKA SLOW COOK UNTIL TENDER AND FALLING APART

As disconsolate Australian fielders try to come to terms with the sudden undismissability of England's batters, Mike Hussey deposits a fatigued Michael Clarke in his new fielding position.

England arrived at the Gabba in 2010 feeling that it wasn't a ground they'd really been getting on with in recent years.

The two parties hadn't exactly been BFFs in the 1990s, but since the millennium things had really turned nasty. The last time they'd toured, in 2006, Australia had put on 9/602 and England had responded with 157. The time before that, Nasser Hussain had invited Australia to bat and Australia had graciously accepted that invitation and blithely sashayed[1] to 1/339.

The general feeling was that while you couldn't technically lose the Ashes in the first Test, you could certainly erect some very clear signage indicating which way things were definitely going to go.

All too aware of this, the 2010 vintage tourists saw their captain, Andrew Strauss, dismissed in the first over of the series, after which they awkwardly made their way to 4/172 at tea on the first day. Not great, but not terrible either, given that start. The home team – and crowd – were at least relatively quiet now. If the English could keep things calm, they stood a chance of making a halfway decent total.

Immediately after tea they surrendered a hat-trick to Peter Siddle. On – as Mark Taylor on commentary so memorably bellowed – his birthday.

Not too long after that, they were all out for a very-obviously-unsatisfactory 260, and by the end of day two, Mike Hussey and Brad Haddin had made a start on what would become a 307-run partnership. It was all very familiar, and by stumps on day three England were 0/19 in their second innings – still 202 runs behind.

It was very definitely all happening again.

What happened next was experienced in markedly different ways depending on whether you were in Australia or England. Australians saw events unfold in real time, and it quickly became annoying, then boring, then super-irritating. Why weren't England collapsing like normal? Fully expecting England to collapse like normal, and shorn of any motivation to endure another late night, Britons, for the most part, went to bed, awash

---

1   Okay, Matthew Hayden's blithe sashaying isn't quite like other people's blithe sashaying – but these things are relative.

with dread at the prospect of that first scorecard check in the morning.

It might not immediately appear this way, but that second way of experiencing things was much, much weirder.

Imagine you start watching a very derivative and awful film, the kind of late-night, low-budget monstrosity where every word of dialogue is a cliché and every plot development is a tired old trope you've seen a thousand times before.

You see the off-the-rails loose cannon detective who doesn't need a partner called into the captain's office. He really shouldn't have gone into that warehouse without backup. Why can't he do things by the book? The captain bawls him out and demands his badge. Auto-completing the film and finding nothing else worthy of your attention, your brain sends you to sleep.

When you awake some hours later, the detective is getting archery lessons from a tiny bipedal hippopotamus, while the ghost of his captain is making wisecracks from the sidelines.

Um, what? Everything you thought you knew has been detonated in an instant.

What happened on day four at the Gabba was that England, careering as they were towards inevitable defeat, somehow went through an entire day of Test cricket losing only one wicket. Given their history and the situation they'd got themselves into, this was nothing short of inexplicable.

Bleary-eyed Britons struggled to parse the data. Two openers had been batting and now, a full day's play later, one of those openers was batting with the number three. Had it rained? Had England performed so badly they'd been obliged to bat a third time? No. They were just still batting. And then, the next day, they carried on.

The final (match-saving) tally was 1/517, with contributions of 110 from Andrew Strauss, 135 not out from Jonathan Trott and a barely credible 235 not out from Alastair Cook.

'Well, that was one of the all-time weirdest one-off freak innings,' concluded absolutely everybody who had seen even five minutes of Ashes cricket Down Under in the last twenty years. Except then they did it again in the very next Test, at Adelaide.

This time Australia batted first, making 245 all out, which suggested a more challenging pitch. But after losing Strauss for a single run, England responded with four century partnerships in a row. Cook settled for a mere 148 on this occasion, while Kevin Pietersen top-scored with 227.

When England were twice skittled for under 200 in Perth to bring the series score back to 1–1, normal service appeared to have resumed.

Nope. In the fourth Test it was Trott's turn again, his 168 not out a full 70 runs more than all of Australia's batters combined had managed on day one (a day that, honestly, could warrant its own chapter in a book such as this).

Next Test? Cook was at it again with 189, while Ian Bell and Matt Prior chipped in with what almost felt like afterthought hundreds towards the end of what was an incredibly long series if you were an Australian bowler. Peter Siddle, who played all five Tests, must have felt like he was due another birthday.

Because what these bare run tallies do not in any way capture is the sheer, breathtaking lack of urgency on display on most of these occasions.

Cook's 235 at the Gabba took ten and a half hours. Strauss batted for four of those hours and Trott for the other six. In his next innings, Cook batted for seven hours and didn't even break a sweat. No, literally – while Pietersen changed his gloves regularly, Cook somehow remained in the same pair. 'I tell people it's my fitness,' he said later, 'but it's not quite true. I was born this way. I'm just not very sweaty.'

Cook's final innings of the series took another eight hours. That got him to 766 runs in seven innings at an average of 127.66. He faced 1438 balls – which is 139 more than his former teammate Steve Harmison faced in his entire 63-Test career.

If there was a single moment that sums up England's batting in this series, however, it was one involving Trott, who particularly irked his opponents with his weird automaton guard-marking routine, which he seemed to indulge in every ball.

At one point wicketkeeper Brad Haddin stepped in and made a big show out of marking Trott's guard for him. Haddin presumably felt that if he could interrupt the batter's routine, he might put him off his game. Trott stood behind him while he did this, staring blankly at the line as if Haddin were invisible.

'You don't have to do one of yours now,' said Haddin, scraping away at the crease with his foot.

Trott continued waiting. When Haddin finally moved away, he stepped forward, methodically drew a line in the dirt in precisely the same spot and made his way to 168 not out (in seven and a half hours).

ACTIVITY CORNER

1. Write a screenplay in which a rogue cop is partnered with a bipedal hippopotamus archer to solve the murder of their captain.
2. Call it *Shooting from the Hippo*.
3. Make it gritty and realistic.

28

NAT SCIVER-BRUNT SCORES A RESULT-ALTERING TON

AKA THE BITTER PATTERN OF (NOT SO) TINY FEATS

As any half-decent probability theorist will tell you, correlation does not imply causation. (Although, having said that, the fact that the two concepts are so often bandied about together surely suggests that we need to delve more deeply into how they *are* related. Ha! No. Just a little meta-joke there for the true probability theory-heads. Testify, stats-savvy siblings.)

Nevertheless, cricketers are a superstitious lot, and if they spot any kind of pattern between their actions and on-field outcomes, they'll tend to lean into it.

Often those patterns have no rational justification but are adhered to anyway. If anybody moves from their spot in the dressing room, we'll lose a wicket. If I swap the bails before I bowl the next ball, I'll take a wicket. If I fidget endlessly and touch every part of my body before I face up, I'll stake a claim to being the best batter since Bradman. And so on.

Sometimes, though, those patterns *are* actual causation. If I play better cricket than my opponents – score more runs, bowl more wicket-taking deliveries, hold onto more catches, review idiotic umpiring decisions more wisely – then I will tend to have better cricket results. Nothing superstitious about that. Playing good cricket that results in a winning outcome is unremarkable.

What *is* remarkable, however, is the situation Nat Sciver-Brunt found herself in, heading into the final match of the 2023 Women's Ashes.

Over an eighteen-month period, Sciver-Brunt had proven herself to be the pre-eminent thorn in Australia's side. (Not that she was in Australia's side, of course. She was in England's side, as per standard ICC national qualification protocols.)

Since the end of the 2021/22 Ashes, Sciver-Brunt had played Australia in four ODIs. In three of those matches, she'd scored magnificent unbeaten centuries. She was, in fact, the only cricketer in the world to have scored a ton against Australia in either white-ball format since 2019.

And every time she did so, England had been beaten.

The first of her centuries had come in both teams' opening match of the 2022 Women's ODI World Cup. Rachael Haynes and Meg Lanning had combined for a 196-run partnership on the way to Australia scoring 3/310. Sciver (as she was known at the time) had come to the crease following captain Heather Knight's dismissal in the 19th over of the chase and kept England in the hunt. Heading into the final over alongside fiancée Katherine Brunt, the soon-to-be Sciver-Brunts needed 16 runs to win. Jess Jonassen, however, kept the scoring to three and took the last two wickets, leaving Sciver stranded on 109.

As great a knock as that had been, Sciver somehow topped it in her next match against Australia, which happened to be the World Cup final. This time Alyssa Healy had performed her classic trick of 'I'm going to single-handedly win a World Cup final' (another fun little cricketing hobby shared between spouses, given that Healy's husband, Mitchell Starc, had effectively ended New Zealand's hopes of winning the 2015 Men's ODI World Cup Final by bowling captain/talisman Brendon McCullum in his first over). Healy scored a record 170 from 138 balls as Australia amassed 5/356 from their 50 overs. Sciver, apparently oblivious to the fact that Healy had already won the match with her breathtaking innings, decided that she'd quite like to win the match with a breathtaking innings of her own. She smashed 148 not out from 121 balls, impossibly keeping England on track to complete what would have been the greatest ever World Cup final run chase. Unfortunately for Sciver, however, everybody else was dismissed for 27 or fewer and Australia held on to win.

The third of the by-now-hyphenated Sciver-Brunt's centuries came in the penultimate match of the 2023 Ashes, in Southampton. England needed a win to keep the series alive, but Australia had scored 7/282, thanks to an Ellyse Perry 91 and Georgia Wareham flat-batting 26 off the final over. Again, Sciver-Brunt marshalled the run chase, scoring 111 not out from 99 balls. This time she headed into the final over needing 15 runs for victory, but Jonassen defended the total once more, retaining the Ashes for Australia via a three-run victory.

And that was where things stood entering the final match of the 2023 Women's Ashes. Three ODI centuries for Sciver-Brunt in her last four matches. All three (individually) undefeated. All three in defeats.

Now, obviously there was a rational explanation for this. Namely, that this was an Australian side that mostly didn't lose, particularly in ODIs. This was a side that paid little heed to its thorn, no matter how prickly and stunning that thorn's batting form might have been.

But 'mostly didn't lose' means Australia did sometimes lose. They had, as it so happened, lost the first match of the ODI leg of the Ashes series. This, of course, was the one ODI out of Sciver-Brunt's previous four against Australia where she hadn't scored an unbeaten century, dismissed instead for 31.

This was trend enough to raise superstitious eyebrows, regardless of any team statisticians yammering on about correlation and causation. Should Australia always allow Sciver-Brunt to score centuries? It was a seemingly crazy tactic but also an effective one. Was this how cricket worked now?

Ellyse Perry was taking no chances, having apparently bought entirely into the notion that a team's leading all-rounder notching a ton might be perilous (or, indeed, Perry-lous). In addition to her 91 in the second ODI, Perry had responded to being dismissed for 99 in the Test that opened the series with cool indifference. (Easy to muster such indifference, one imagines, when losing your wicket still means your Test batting average remains in the mid-70s.)

Unconvinced by the cowardly forces of rationality, the Australians locked in their plan for the final ODI of the series. England batted first and Sciver-Brunt made yet another century, her fourth in five matches, scoring 129 out of a total of 9/285, to leave the tourists bursting with confidence at the innings break. Instead, they were inexplicably bowled out for 199 in the 36th over to give England victory by 86 runs. As has become modern Ashes tradition, an Australian side had come to England and retained the urn, but left without a series win.[1]

More importantly, Sciver-Brunt's silly pattern of losing to Australia every time she scored a century had been broken. As a reward, she was named Player of the Match, Player of the ODI Series, joint Player of the Ashes Series (alongside Ash 'it's short for Ashes-dominating' Gardner) and the number one ODI batter in the world.

All these awards were both correlated with *and* caused by her staggering run of ODI batting form.

---

1   In contrast, the next women's Ashes, in 2025, would see England come to Australia and not merely fail to regain the urn, but depart without winning a single match. The 16–0 clean sweep was a mishmash of horrors for Heather Knight's side, featuring dreadful fielding and clueless batting. On the plus side, coach Jon Lewis tapped into some magnificently absurd excuse-offering, culminating in the bizarre claim that Australia's dominance was due to the number of people he spotted on the beach in Bondi and Coogee.

Nat Sciver-Brunt, visibly concerned that her century has just cost England the match.

27

NASSER ASKS AUSTRALIA TO BAT

AKA WHO GIVES A TOSS?

We've all made decisions we later regretted. It's just that most of us haven't had to stand under the harsh Queensland sun for an entire day while the full span of our misjudgement has slowly but relentlessly unfurled, with countless cricket fans watching on and marvelling at (or fulminating about) exactly how much of a moron we are.

'We're gonna have a bowl,' said Nasser Hussain after the coin toss for the first Test of the 2002/03 Ashes at Brisbane. 'It was a bit of a difficult one. You know, conditions here – there's a bit of grass on the wicket, and I just want to give our attack the best chance to get into the Australian batting line-up.'

Quick spoiler here: on day one of the 2002 Gabba Test, the England attack very much did not 'get into' the Australian batting line-up. Some of the things it did get into included trouble, the record books and, in the case of one player, an ambulance.

It's not always obvious what to do at the toss, and there isn't often a right and a wrong option. Generally, as a captain, you make your choice, you play the game and then it's only at some point during the fourth innings that everyone decides the defeat is all down to your terrible call.

When a captain calls correctly but feels torn between their two options, that feeling of being torn suggests the batting or bowling advantages inherent to the pitch aren't immediately obvious. In particular, it suggests it isn't the kind of pitch where bowling means spending a whole day retrieving the ball from the boundary. Even on the rare occasions when that has happened, it hasn't tended to be a day as high-profile as the first of an Ashes series.

Hussain had spied some grass and concluded there would be 'a bit in it' in the first session. Sure enough, England did indeed get a breakthrough – Justin Langer, caught behind off Simon Jones for 32. The problem was that it wasn't until Australia had reached 339 that they got a second wicket.

That late dismissal – Ricky Ponting for 123, not long before stumps – was, alas, not to Jones, because with the score reading 1/139 the Welshman had tried to slide and stop the ball at mid-on, only for his boot to catastrophically stick in the turf. Fielding at mid-off, Hussain said he heard the crack.

As Jones was carried from the field by Steve Harmison and Jason Gillespie, one home fan took the trouble to inform him he was 'a weak Pommie bastard'. An Australian anterior cruciate ligament would of course have remained unruptured had it been subjected to the same forces.

Jones didn't return to the team for another eighteen months.

Along with being effectively one man up, Australia also ended that first day on 2/364, which meant that what little hope England fans had harboured – and it really was very little, having lost every Ashes series since 1989 – was all but extinguished just one day into the series.

'I thought there was something in the wicket first up and I wanted to give our bowlers something to work with,' said Hussain. 'As you see, when it gets flat, it's very difficult to bowl them out. So I read it wrong, and you hold your hands up and you move on from there.'

But do you move on? Do you really? Every four years, there is a coin toss ahead of an Ashes Test at the Gabba, and whenever that happens, everyone looks at Nasser Hussain and raises a knowing eyebrow.

Hussain has been sighing and laughing self-deprecatingly about this for twenty-odd years now. His commentary stints will be intermittently peppered with references to Brisbane until the day he finally hangs up his mic.

You probably don't ever truly move on from starting an Ashes series like this.

Of course, while Hussain was in many ways the MVP of this particular farrago, it's not enough to simply make a bad decision. If you're lumbered with good enough players, they can undo even the most misguided decision at the toss. To make day one of the 2002 Gabba Test a classic, England's bowlers and fielders also had to deliver.

Jones's horrific injury certainly helped in this regard, as did the knee injury that had sent Darren Gough home just days before the series began. Ashley Giles emerged as England's standout bowler from that first innings, finishing with figures of 4/101. Ashley Giles was many things, but if he's your best bowler on day one at the Gabba, you've got some problems.

'Rarely, if ever, has the first session of an Ashes campaign begun without one bouncer being bowled in anger,' wrote Steve Waugh in his autobiography. 'It was tame, lame stuff that allowed Matthew Hayden and Ricky Ponting to take the match beyond England's reach after just two sessions of play and set the mood for the whole series.'

England's fielding was similarly exceptional. Hayden was dropped four times on his way to 186 not out at the close of play.

'I believe we're going to have a bowl, bowl it in the right areas and take our catches,' Hussain had said when justifying his decision to bowl. At the end of the game – apparently having grown about eight days' worth of stubble in just four days – he revisited that belief. 'Er, yeah, I mean, the first day was diabolical, to be honest,' he concluded. 'Make no mistake of it. Our catching – you know, real dollies – and putting the ball in the right areas and stuff. We were outplayed and we were poor.'

The batting wasn't too great either. They got weirdly closer to Australia's eventual 492 than anyone expected (a mere 167-run deficit was quite the triumph, given that first day), which is presumably what persuaded Steve Waugh to later set them 464 to win.

England fell a little way short of that target: all out for 79 in barely two hours.

But while the performance had ended up an all-round horror show, Hussain wasn't about to allow his contribution at the outset to be forgotten. Speaking after the game, he said: 'I'm first to admit when I got things wrong, and however this game had gone – even if we'd won it by some fluke at the end – I'd still say I got the toss wrong here.'

His teammates apparently agreed. Writing in his autobiography, Hussain recalled the atmosphere at the end of that first day thus: 'We were very quiet that evening in the dressing room. Somebody said, "Is it still doing a bit, skip?" but nobody laughed.'

Steve Waugh attempts to beckon down a hovering pterodactyl (just out of shot).

26
ENGLAND LACK WHEELS

AKA BOWLIN', BOWLIN', BOLAND

Where, exactly, did the wheels come off in England's 2021/22 Ashes campaign?

There are some England fans (and players!) who pinpoint the decision to tour in the first place as the moment, given the heavy Covid-19 restrictions in place in Australia at the time. 'All well and good for other nations to tour our green and pleasant kingdom during these pandemic times,' seemed to be the logic. 'But to have our lads reciprocate? Be reasonable.'

Of course, the simple idea of refusing to play the Ashes in Australia would have saved England fans a lot of disappointment over the past thirty years. So you can see the appeal.

Once England made the dumb mistake of embarking on an Ashes tour, though, it's possible the wheels were detached as early as the warm-up matches against an England Lions XI. The Brisbane weather conspired to wash out all but 29 overs of the first three-day match. The second, a four-day match, almost got a full day of play in. Based on these trends, a third match, had it existed and been scheduled to take place over, say, fifteen to eighteen days, might have just about provided sufficient preparation for the first Test. Unluckily for England, this third match's shortness of length and lack of existence went against them.

Another thing that went against England as they approached the first Test – and another early candidate for the moment of wheel disengagement – was the decision to not select their two most experienced bowlers. As we discussed in No. 36, James Anderson and Stuart Broad were instead sent off to explore the great tourist attractions of Brisbane (the Story Bridge, the King Wally Lewis Statue, the other end of the Story Bridge) while the rest of the team played.

Rory Burns being bowled first ball of the series, and the ensuing collapse (3/11, 5/60, 8/122, all out 147 – choose your dismantling poison) that set up a first Test defeat by nine wickets? Just a few more points where one might detect some dislodging of wheels.

Assuming, however, that you're of the mind that the worst that can happen to one's wheels one Test into a five-match series is some severe loosening, the lead-up to the second Test offered hope for England. Australia's new captain, Pat Cummins, was ruled out of the Test having carelessly dined in a restaurant near one of the twenty-five people in the entire state of South Australia who had tested positive to the virus at the time. Josh Hazlewood was out with a series-ending side strain. Anderson and Broad were back for England to bowl under lights in the day/night Test. Any rickety England wheels from the Gabba drubbing were surely having their nuts tightened heading into Adelaide.

Also having his nuts tightened? England captain Joe Root, who was hit in the boxless testicles during warm-ups prior to the fourth day's play. Root was sent to hospital for scans and missed the first hour's play, with Ben Stokes taking over captaincy duties (if you can imagine such a thing).

By that stage of the Test, England's wheels were rather wobbly once more. Australia were 282 in front with nine wickets in hand, Jos Buttler was fumbling regulation catches off Marnus Labuschagne, and Ollie Robinson was about to start inexplicably bowling off-spin. To ensure maximum wobbliness, a ruthless Mitchell Starc hit Root in the nuts once more in the final session, then took his wicket.[1] England closed out the day 386 runs short of victory with six wickets remaining.

While England had no chance of winning the Test, Buttler strove to redeem his earlier fumbling glovework. England's greatest white-ball batter therefore eschewed his usual big-hitting explosiveness and instead played for the draw, batting for more than two sessions and 200 balls for an absurdly uncharacteristic 26 runs. Ridiculous in itself, but made only more so when he was the penultimate wicket of the match, treading on his stumps as he defended a Jhye Richardson delivery to point. Oblivious to the jeering, zinging bail behind him, Buttler contemplated a single, before delighted, celebrating Australian fielders ruined his evening in a way that only delighted, celebrating Australian fielders can.

Two-nil down then, with Root having further salt rubbed into his wounds (best not to visualise this) by Labuschagne replacing him as the number-one-ranked Test batter. England's wheels were dangling at the very end of their axles.

Enter the human lug wrench, Scott Boland.

There were only a couple of overs left in the second day of the MCG Test when Boland was thrown the ball for the first time in England's second innings. Root was at the crease,

---

1   Not a euphemism.

England 60 runs behind. One solid day of batting on the third day of the Test could get them back into not just the match but the series.

Instead, finally, unequivocally, the wheels came off.

With the frenetic precision of a Formula One pit crew, Boland opened his second-innings account with the wicket of Haseeb Hameed third ball, caught behind. Two balls later, the nightwatching Jack Leach left a ball that hit the top of off stump.

Despite his success at the end of the second day, Boland (2/1 off one over) wasn't given the ball again until the 11th over of the third day. By then, England had moved from 4/31 to 5/56, with Stokes the man out.

Jonny Bairstow was first to fall in Boland's new spell, LBW to a double-umpire's-call decision on the fifth ball of his first over of the day (3/5 off two overs).

Next over, MCG-Lovin' (the name on his fake ID) found Root's edge, and David Warner held the catch at slip (4/5 off three overs).

Boland completed his five-wicket haul first ball of his next over, smartly pouching a return catch from Wood. He tossed the ball away before picking it back up and bashfully raising it to the crowd for a celebratory split-second. The 19 balls it had taken him to snare five wickets was the equal fastest in Test history. (We'll get to Stuart Broad at Trent Bridge soon enough.) Two balls later, Boland had six, with Robinson caught by Labuschagne at slip.

Boland finished with 6/7 off four overs. Bay 13 bowed in homage to the effort. Commentators called for statues to be built. The Johnny Mullagh Medal for Player of the Match in the Boxing Day Test was awarded to a fellow Indigenous cricketer. England were all out for 68. The Ashes were decided.

Boland had not only removed the wheels, but he'd stripped bare the entire England cricket machinery, leaving only a husk rusting away in the middle of the MCG.

All things considered, it was a half-decent Test debut. To paraphrase that legendary enthusiast of wheel-optional cars, *Back to the Future*'s Doc Brown: 'Great, Scott!'

Scott Boland in a rare non-wicket-taking moment.

25

AUSTRALIA CELEBRATE A DRAW

AKA BRETT LEE: SAVIOUR, SURVIVALIST, CENTRE OF ATTENTION

Brett Lee ponders the unwelcome prospect of being asked to save Australia with the bat twice in two Tests.

If you needed someone to bat for your life, who would you pick? People usually go for a cussed pragmatist like Geoffrey Boycott or Allan Border. Maybe Shivnarine Chanderpaul would get a look-in, or Rahul Dravid.

Weirdly, no one ever goes for Brett Lee, despite his track record in the highest-stakes moments being second to none – which is surely what you're after in this bizarre and vanishingly unlikely hypothetical scenario.[1]

It is one of the peculiar and best features of Test cricket that its moments of greatest tension more frequently involve not its finest batters but those who would more likely count themselves among the worst.

In August 2005, Lee found himself with a weekly appointment for excruciatingly gut-twisting Ashes Test climaxes.

If 'a thing that happened in real life that you definitely already know about' can ever be considered a spoiler, then ... spoiler alert! Lee was a central figure at Edgbaston for an event we'll be covering later in this book. He, Shane Warne and Michael Kasprowicz got within three runs of victory in the second Test, when they put on an unlikely 104 runs for Australia's final two wickets.

The specific scenario he and Kasprowicz eventually found themselves in – where success or failure in a Test match feels like it hinges on the outcome of a single delivery – is as rare as it is agonising for anyone with an interest in the outcome. Usually, at the moment a given match is decided, there are overs, sessions, perhaps even days left unused. That fact unavoidably diminishes the tension. Watching on, you don't feel so much is at stake, because whatever happens with the next ball, the outcome is generally already predictable.

The difference that August Sunday at Edgbaston was that, right down to the final delivery, no one knew what the result was going to be. A lot of specialist Test batters never face such a scenario in their entire careers. Brett Lee, a half-decent number nine, only had to wait until the following Sunday to experience it again.

---

1   For one thing, to even begin to decide which batter you'd entrust with this macabre responsibility, you'd need far more information on how the entire process works. Is it some kind of *Saw* deathtrap? Perhaps triggered by Zing bails? Can you bribe the bowler to consistently overstep? More information, please.

The third Test of the 2005 Ashes took place at Old Trafford and saw Glenn McGrath returned to the side at number eleven in the wake of (spoiler alert!) Kasprowicz's abject failure in that key batting position.

McGrath's presence and Shane Warne's 600th Test wicket couldn't, however, prevent England from making 444 in their first innings, with captain Michael Vaughan contributing 166. In their reply, Australia were hit by a fresh burst of reverse swing from old-ball specialist Simon Jones, who took 6/53 after three of the top four had been swiftly prised out with the new ball by, um, Ashley Giles. Jones's wickets included arch competitor Shane Warne for 90 – the only batter to exceed the extras tally of 38.

Australia's final score of 302 meant England had a 142-run lead. Only McGrath threatened the English batters as they cantered towards a declaration, and even he conceded almost a run a ball as he took five wickets. Andrew Strauss was the centurion this time around, and England's 6/280 towards the end of the fourth day's play meant Australia needed 423 to win – a target that was down to 399 by the close without the loss of any wickets.

Tickets aren't usually sold in advance for the fifth day of a Test match because there's no guarantee that such a thing will exist. There are various estimates as to how many people tried and failed to get into Old Trafford for that fifth day's play. Somewhere around 20,000 seems to be the consensus, all left roaming the streets like sad, esky-carrying zombies in sun visors (the picnicking dead), not knowing quite what to do with themselves.

The scale of this exclusion was symbolic of how things had been building over the summer and indeed the preceding years. Fans in England felt like the 2005 Ashes was going to be a Big Deal and the Edgbaston finish had only encouraged this notion. However, those who did get in were given a reminder just how difficult it was to beat Australia at this time.

Key to this was Ricky Ponting, who played one of those innings that seems to have been wrongly forced into a match, like a sky-blue jigsaw piece hammered into an overwhelmingly muddy brown puzzle (not one of the more aesthetically pleasing jigsaws, this one). As his partners came and went, Ponting was unfazed – just as he was unfazed by the pitch, the bowling and the situation.

At 7/340, Australia needed 83 runs for victory, and English minds understandably went back to the previous Test.

It is, of course, a tall order to score 83 runs with your last three wickets, but a Test series constructs context as it goes along, framing events in terms of what has gone before. It had only been a week since Australia's last two wickets had scored more than was needed here.

However, when 7/340 became 8/340 at the fall of Warne (freakishly caught by keeper Geraint Jones via the knee of Strauss at second slip), the chance of an Australian victory receded. With the loss of that wicket and the arrival of Lee, flinging of bat and deployment of long handle no longer seemed like sensible options. Nevertheless, while there wasn't enough time for an Australia win, the tension remained, because the ticking clock meant there were still two possible results. The draw seemed the more likely outcome until Ponting fell for 156 with four overs to go.

Now, a tenth-wicket partnership will often last four overs. It's a bit different when it has to, though. The worth of Ponting's peerless fifth-day anomaly of a knock and Warne's indomitable efforts earlier in the match (the first-innings defiance with the bat and four wickets with the ball) were now wholly dependent on whether Brett Lee and Glenn McGrath could keep the ball out for the next twenty minutes.

For 23 deliveries, Lee and McGrath did precisely that, Lee carelessly hitting boundaries from the final balls of the fourth-last and second-last overs, denying himself the strike. McGrath, however, did not do a Kasprowicz on him, successfully keeping Steve Harmison at bay and even hitting a pointless boundary of his own.

Come the final ball, England still needed that one final wicket. Unlike a week earlier, Lee was at the striker's end. This time, he was in control of what would happen. Harmison went for the yorker, but sent it down a little too full. Lee, for some reason, saw fit to clip it to the fine-leg boundary for four final unnecessary runs.[2]

Gratuitous boundaries aside, the main job was done. The man who had deflated to his knees at Edgbaston as if one of his valves had gone could celebrate this time.

---

[2] Boosting his career average by 0.05 – a fitting reward for being put through such hell in two consecutive matches.

Australia were elated. They'd battled the odds for hours and hours and had been but a crap forward defensive away from defeat.

Conversely, England were dispirited. Slogging away, getting so close and being denied – it was like designing and building the perfect home only to be told that planning permission had been revoked on the day you were about to move in.

Before the Old Trafford Test, the series score was 1–1. After the Old Trafford Test, the score was still 1–1. Totally disconnected from events, one might ask: 'Why bother? What was the point of all of that?'

As the Australians celebrated earning a draw, Vaughan gathered his men, who had suffered the same result. 'Look at them celebrating mere survival,' was the gist of what he said to them.

Why would the unstoppable, unconquerable Australian team be happy with a draw against England, whom they had routinely bullied for series after series? There is no way of answering that question without coming to see that Aussie dynasty in a different light. While the scoreline remained the same, this is what had changed over the course of the third Test.

As such, there was cause for optimism for the home team. But at the same time, if they were to win the series, they would have to find a way past Lee, the one batter who had emerged unbeaten after two of the highest-tension finishes in Ashes history. (Spoiler: they did.)

Make no mistake, if you ever need someone to bat for your life, Brett Lee's your man. Failing that (if Lee's a bit busy that day – if the gutters need clearing or he's got some shelves to put up, say), then your second choice must surely be Glenn McGrath.

24

MICHAEL SLATER IS RUN OUT BUT NOT OUT

AKA SUCH A PROBLEM

Michael Slater suffers a temporary outbreak of Bannermania.

One of the most ridiculous aspects of Ashes cricket traces all the way back to the very first Test: a record set by Charles Bannerman in 1877, and yet to be broken. (At the time of writing, at least.[1])

The Bannerman record is, of course, the record for the highest proportion of runs scored by a single batter in a completed team innings. As mentioned in No. 46, in the first ever Test, the first ever Australian opener scored an unbeaten 165 to contribute the majority of the first ever Australian Test team's first ever first innings total of 245. That's 67.34 per cent of the runs. No man has ever beaten that percentage. (Although one woman has – England's Enid Bakewell scored an unbeaten 112 of the team's 164 against the West Indies in 1979 – 68.29 per cent.[2])

On the men's front, however, the closest anybody has come to knocking off Bannerman was Michael Slater in the fifth Test of the 1998/99 Ashes.

It was a Test overflowing with nonsense. Mark Taylor completed a tosswash against Alec Stewart, winning his fifth coinflip of the series, a feat for which he would soon be named Australian of the Year, triggering his retirement from Test cricket; he had no more worlds left to conquer, presumably.

Shane Warne, out injured all summer, returned alongside the man for whom the ground was named, SCG MacGill. Stuart Charles Glyndwr would outshine his more acclaimed (and less interestingly named) leg-spinning partner, taking a dozen wickets in the Test, compared to Shane Keith's mere two. One of those 12 MacGill wickets, the final one of the Test, was Peter Such, caught and bowled in comical fashion after Such drilled the ball into the ankle of a recoiling Slater, only for it (the ball, not the ankle) to rebound straight to the bowler.

Outshining leg-spinners Warne and MacGill on the spinning track of Sydney, however, was England non-spinner Darren Gough. The first day of the Test concluded with

---

1   Quick peek behind the curtain: whenever one writes about the seeming unassailability of Bannerman's record, there is always a period of authorial nervousness between when the book is written and when it hits the shelves. Needless concern, of course, because Bannerman invariably holds off all contenders.
2   She also took 10/75 in that game, as well as making 68 in the first innings – so, you know, a pretty solid performance. It was her final Test.

the Australian lower order being administered a triple-dose of Gough medicine, as the Yorkshireman took the first Ashes hat-trick by an England bowler in a hundred years. It was part of a collapse of 5/3 in 15 deliveries, and concluded with the exhilarating sight of Gough bursting through the defences of both MacGill and Colin Miller and knocking their stumps everywhere.

In between Gough's hat-trick and MacGill's 12-fer came Slater's pursuit of Bannerman's record.

Australia's first innings total of 322 had been countered by England's 220. But any thoughts the home side had of extending the 102-run lead into hope-crushing territory (a standard Australian ploy in 1990s Ashes Tests) were swiftly unthought.

Instead, Australia mustered just 184 in their second innings, with Mark Waugh gliding his way to 24 before Mark Ramprakash took a smart one-handed catch off Dean Headley. Other than Waugh, however, everybody made single-figures.

Everybody except for Slater, that is, who made triple-figures – 123, to be precise. When he was out, he had Bannerman's record (and, for that matter, Bakewell's) in his grasp, having scored 68.33 per cent of the team's total of 8/180. But Miller and MacGill, two bowlers with either no sense of history or an extreme sense of one, added four runs for the ninth wicket (the tenth wicket included Glenn McGrath, so predictably added zero runs), and Bannerman triumphed once more.

As ridiculous as it was for Slater to get so close to breaking the Bannerman record, however, it was not even close to the most absurd moment of his innings. That came when he was on 35, a mere 58.33 per cent of Australia's total of 2/60. Mark Waugh clipped a ball off Such's bowling down to long-on and called for two, only for the return throw from Headley to directly hit the stumps at the non-striker's end.

Slater was, let's be 100 per cent clear, short of his ground. He'd been dawdling back for the second and hadn't anticipated the accuracy of the throw. His panicked flustling[3] came too late, and the on-field umpire sent it upstairs to confirm.

---

3 *Flustle* (verb), a flustered hustle in which one frantically accelerates part way through taking a run upon realising that, contrary to expectations, the fielder is throwing to your end.

Here's where things became fun/maddening (delete depending on national allegiance).

Because it turned out that there was no single camera angle that showed both Slater out of his ground *and* the stumps being broken. The sole side-on angle was obscured by some Such. The overhead angle was, as with all other cameras at the time, in standard definition, and hence too far away to zoom in with any certainty.

Yes, if you squinted and combined in your mind's eye the evidence from both angles, the obvious conclusion – extremely obvious – was that Slater was out. But third umpire Simon Taufel was having none of this 'mind's eye' gibberish. Why resort to one's imagination when there was a perfectly valid set of playing conditions one could consult instead? If there was no single frame showing both the stumps broken and Slater outside the crease, then Slater was not out.

It was a controversial decision, but, at the time, not one that seemed match-turning. It was only later, after it became clear that Slater would be the only cricketer doing any second-innings scoring for Australia, that the depth of its importance became clear.

Slater added a further 88 runs, helping Australia to a lead of 286. The lead eventually proved 98 too many for England to run down. The Slater run-out not out decision was, indeed, decisive.

As Headley later said, 'I'm not saying we would have won, but it would have been a damn sight closer' had Slater been given out. (Mark Butcher was more adamant: 'I'm 100 per cent sure we'd have won in Sydney had the Slater run-out been given.')

Even crazier? England were coming off a bonkers Test win in Melbourne a week earlier (see No. 43). Victory in this fifth Test would have therefore seen the series level at 2–2.

A 1990s Ashes series where England – a visiting England, no less – finished level with Australia? Why, that's the most ridiculous thing of all.

23

STUART BROAD'S FINAL ACTS

AKA BOWING OUT (AND BOWLING OUT) SIXESSFULLY

There are many different ways to bow out of Test cricket.

James Anderson's final Test wicket (the West Indies' Joshua Da Silva) was an absolute beauty – but it was entirely unclear at the time that it was in fact his final one. He continued bowling and later shelled a caught and bowled chance that would have secured victory.

This meant it was Gus Atkinson who got to take that final match-clinching wicket. When he apologised to Anderson for doing so, Anderson told him to fuck off. The taciturn seamer didn't yearn for some grand finish because – somewhat unfortunately, for a man who took 704 Test wickets – he never really had much appetite for attention.

Earlier in the match, in England's only innings, Jamie Smith was caught on the boundary before Anderson had faced a ball. This meant that the seamer's final act as a Test batter had been to play out a dot ball against India four months earlier, a time when even Jimmy himself didn't know that retirement was looming.

So to sum that up, Anderson's final shot was a forward defensive that resulted in a dot ball. His final delivery was a strangled appeal for LBW and also a dot ball.

In contrast, Stuart Broad's final shot was a six and his final delivery was the wicket that won the fifth Test of the 2023 Ashes.

Broad, it seems fair to say, didn't mind being the centre of attention. Speaking to *The Independent* about stepping out of the limelight a few months after his retirement, he claimed he hadn't been chasing the 'feeling' of wickets and of the crowd cheering.

'How do I replace that?' he asked. 'Maybe I don't need to replace that. Maybe I don't need to chase that feeling of that pure adulation.'

As open-ended musings go, the wording of this one seemed incriminating. Make no mistake, Stuart Broad loved the attention.

Over the years, his batting in particular came to demand it. It's not that he improved – his overall ability with the bat actually deteriorated markedly after he top-edged a Varun Aaron bouncer into his own face in 2014. Before that broken nose and the resultant surgery and nightmares, there had been intermittent talk that Broad might one day be considered an all-rounder. At that point he had a Test hundred and ten fifties to his name and there was a crispness to some of his strokeplay that suggested he was capable of much more.

Ben Stokes takes delight in yet another outrageous piece of Stuart Broad Mischief™.

You know how it is, though – an utterly decimated face can dampen almost anyone's enthusiasm. When he returned to Test cricket, he had transformed into a (quite justifiably) cowardly tailender who backed away from even the full balls.

This moment was, however, the making of Broad the batting entertainer. Over time, he reintroduced all his best shots, and while these displaced a great many adequate and unremarkable strokes, they did not for some reason squeeze out any of the wild, panicked hitting he'd honed in the meantime.

The end result was a man whose innings delivered the greatest density of excitement imaginable. Broad's method became an exquisite blend of woeful shot selection and panic, underpinned by weirdly good hand–eye coordination. This meant that a freakishly high percentage of the deliveries he faced resulted in either boundaries or his dismissal. A lot of the time it was hard to predict which you were watching even as he was playing the shot – or quite often even after he'd hit it.

Anything could happen, but no innings was likely to last too long. The average Stuart Broad innings was absolutely unmissable entertainment, the feeling of impermanence only intensifying the impact of each boundary.

At the centre of all this was the Broad hook shot – a stroke he deployed frequently, brilliantly and awfully.

Right up until that very final shot, Broad remained afraid of the bouncer – terrified, in fact, so much so that he almost could not help but larrup it into the stands for six. Broad was a cornered tiger with the short ball, lashing out with fear in his eyes and scary retractable knives protruding from his furry, stripy fingers.

As Mitchell Starc dug in that final delivery, Broad responded as he had done so many times before – by flinching and ducking and hitting the ball, all at the same time. On this occasion it went for six, but it would really have been no less fitting had he skied it and been caught out.

At the non-striker's end, James Anderson saw what had happened and knew that it was good. He duly missed a reverse sweep in the next over to ensure that the six would be Broad's final shot.

But there was still much bowling to be done.

The series score was 2–1 to Australia, who now needed 384 to win. After 90.5 overs, they had reached 8/329 and Broad had 0/62 to his name off 18.5 overs.

Broad says that Ben Stokes had already told him this was to be his last over of the spell – and thus, most likely, the last of his career – because he wanted to bring Mark Wood on.

Broad prepared for that final ball the same way anyone would have: by swapping the bails over at the non-striker's end.

Earlier, during one unusually tedious stretch of Australia's first innings, Broad – who was only fielding at the time – had swapped the bails over on the basis that he'd heard from someone that it was 'an Aussie change of luck thing'.[1] Marnus Labuschagne edged Wood to Joe Root at slip next ball. 'I randomly went and celebrated with [non-striker Usman Khawaja] for some reason,' Broad recalled afterwards.[2]

So it was that, apparently unaware of lightning's famed aversion to returning to old haunts, Broad tried this move again ahead of what was scheduled to be his final delivery.

Todd Murphy edged behind.

That would have been a grand way to finish, but a mere wicket was not quite grand enough. Seeing that Broad was seemingly now imbued with real, actual magic, Stokes made the logical decision to give him another over or two. Alex Carey was not immune, which meant that Broad's final delivery became not merely an Australian wicket but a match-winning, series-levelling one.

Over the course of his career, Broad had excelled in all three major areas of ridiculousness, delivering both ridiculously good and ridiculously bad cricket, as well as more than his fair share of ridiculously ridiculous cricket. The only question, therefore, was which of these subcategories he'd bow out with. In combining a perfect batting exit with a perfect bowling one, and having apparently made up and successfully employed a daft new superstition earlier in the match, he arguably delivered two out of three.

---

1   This 'Aussie change of luck thing' was a new one to most Aussies. Possibly all of them.
2   The celebrations were, presumably, not reciprocated.

22

CHRIS ROGERS IS LBW TO GRAEME SWANN

AKA THE WORST PIECE OF CRICKET IN TEST HISTORY

Chris Rogers batting with the serene dignity afforded to only the very few.

Most of the time when we're talking about ridiculous moments in cricket, there are two contrasting views of it. Was that a ridiculously bad collapse by the England bats or a ridiculously great spell of fast bowling by Mitchell Johnson? Was that a ridiculously bad collapse by Australia or a ridiculously skilful spell of bowling by Stuart Broad? Was that a ridiculously scary collapse by Steve Smith or a ridiculously fearsome short ball by Jofra Archer? And so on.

Usually, the most satisfyingly comedic way to look at a moment is from the perspective of the underperforming player(s). Yes, it's fun to gasp in awe at virtuoso cricketing feats, but at some point there's little to be gained from reiterating, 'Hey, that Ian Botham fella is a pretty handy cricketer, isn't he?' It's why you'll often hear commentators say that they're 'running out of superlatives' for a player performing at the peak of their powers.

In contrast, you almost never hear them say that they're running out of pejoratives for those at the nadir. There's always something new to be said about ridiculously dreadful cricket.

The power of dreadful cricket is what makes Chris Rogers's LBW to Graeme Swann in the first innings of the second Test of the 2013 Ashes so comically perfect. There's no need to weigh up whether the absurdity of what happened was the result of ridiculously good cricket by one player or ridiculously bad cricket by their opponent. No. *Everybody* involved in this dismissal played horrible, horrible cricket, to the extent that Swann immediately claimed, in the press conference at the end of the day, that it was 'the worst piece of cricket in Test history'. Low praise indeed!

Swann bowled 15,349 balls in Test cricket. This was surely the worst of them. In the 16th over of Australia's innings, shortly after lunch on the second day, the visitors were 1/50 in reply to England's 361 all out. Swann, bowling his third over, felt the ball slip from his fingers at the top of his action. The result was a loopy full toss that floated gently through the air to Rogers, who'd made his way to a sedate 15 from 44 balls.

Rogers faced 3982 balls in Test cricket. Again, we haven't indulged in a full rewatch but it's safe to suggest the shot he played to Swann's full toss was the ungainliest of his career. Greedily eyeing it, he swung so hard that his helmet lolloped around his head. His bat, however, did not connect with the ball, and the delivery instead dropped straight onto his box.

Marais Erasmus officiated in the middle for more than 150,000 Test match deliveries across his umpiring career (and cast a lazy eye over another 85,000-odd, while bingeing *Grey's Anatomy* in the third umpire's chair). Now, it's unlikely that giving Rogers out to this missed full toss was the worst decision Erasmus made in that time. The trajectory of the ball was, after all, in the general vicinity of the stumps. Swann suggested at his press conference that 'when it actually hit him, it looked stone dead LBW', and while he was hardly an objective witness, it wasn't crazy at first glance to think about giving it out.

On the other hand, a second, Hawkeye-assisted glance would later show the ball missing the stumps by about six inches, so it wasn't one of Erasmus's more sparkling decisions either. It was, in fact, precisely the kind of verdict that the non-striker should advise the batter to use a review to overturn.

Non-striker Usman Khawaja has faced more than 12,000 balls in Tests, and presumably watched a similar number from the other end. (It turns out that 'number of balls not faced' is not a commonly tracked statistic.) But if it's tricky to determine how many deliveries a batter has spent at the non-striker's end, it's even trickier to rank individual moments of non-striker play, unless they're being mankaded or something. Still, of the dozen thousand or so deliveries Khawaja's probably witnessed from twenty-two yards away, his uninterested shrug of the shoulders when Rogers asked if the LBW decision was worth reviewing must rank somewhere near the bottom.

And why didn't Khawaja at least propose that a review might be worth trying? Because Shane Watson had already burnt one of the two reviews available, of course. Trapped plumb leg before by Tim Bresnan in the last over before lunch, Watson decided that he'd really rather not be out. He therefore pounded optimistic fist to hopeful forearm, before trudging off dejected, with the inevitably rejected review in tow. With only one challenge left, Khawaja didn't want to stick his neck out for Rogers.

So there we are. Awful bowling, terrible batting, bad umpiring and lacklustre batting-partnering-built-on-earlier-dismal-reviewing. Very, very bad cricket from everybody involved.

Furthermore, it was very, very

bad cricket that had resulted in the loss of an Australian wicket. It was the first of six for the session as they stumbled from 1/42 to 7/96, with the Australian batters' weaknesses against the swinging, seaming, spinning and undeviating[1] ball brutally exposed by the England attack. They were eventually all out for 128, with Swann claiming four more wickets, none of which staked any claim to being the worst piece of cricket in Test history.

With England leading by 233, the merciful Alastair Cook chose not to enforce the follow-on, dragging the Test into a profitable fourth day. More importantly, Cook's generosity gave us one last digestif to go with the delicious Rogers wicket.

In England's second innings, Ian Bell sliced Ryan Harris to a diving Steve Smith at gully, where he held a low catch. Except, no. Bell stood his ground and the third umpire detected sufficient doubt for him to bat on.

A controversial-ish decision, but ultimately no big deal. At 4/140, England already had 137 runs more than they needed to win the Test, a buffer they'd balloon beyond 300 before Cook terminated the innings following Joe Root's eventual dismissal for 180.

But the denied gully catch, coming so soon after a denied first slip catch off Stuart Broad in the first Test (wait for it …), proved a breaking point for Australia. Or at least for somebody with access to Cricket Australia's Twitter account.

'That decision sucked ass!' raged @CricketAus, accentuating their feelings with a 'bullshit' hashtag.

The tweet was soon deleted and replaced by an apology. There were promises of investigations, which were followed up a few days later by regrets that the perpetrator was unable to be identified. As per more usual corporate social media protocols, all of these follow-up tweets allowed their '#bullshit' to be subtext.

(Many years later, Brad Haddin took responsibility for the tweet, giving him a valuable extra tale to tell on the speaking circuit. The story Haddin told revolved around media managers 'taking a piss', laptops being left open and eventual fingers being pointed at a blameless Shane Watson. Ha ha ha!

---

1 In particular, the undeviating variant that was the gentle, looping full toss aimed at the testicles.

Great stuff. Of course, the timestamp on the tweet apparently coinciding with Haddin being on the field playing a Test match for Australia does suggest a certain hashtag might once again be in play.)

Nevertheless, the worst piece of official cricket board tweeting in Test history? It's right up there.

> ### ACTIVITY CORNER
>
> Using an officially sanctioned cricket streaming service, go back and watch every single delivery bowled or faced by your least favourite cricketer. Find something negative to say about each ball. Do you ever run out of pejoratives? Why or why not?

21

ENGLAND PICK THE SAME TEAM

AKA THE TEAMS,
THEY AREN'T A-CHANGIN'

The 1997 Ashes began in positively freakish fashion with an England victory, a result that was shaped by the even more freakish phenomenon of a double-hundred from one of their batters.

At the time, England fans were well aware that Nasser Hussain's 207 was the side's first double against Australia since David Gower made one in 1985, but at some basic, cellular level they could sense that it would also be the last until Paul Collingwood's in 2006.

Double-hundreds simply did not happen for England in this era – and most definitely not against Australia.

Even more bizarre was the context. The Aussies had at one point been 8/54 in their first innings before a bit of lower-order whackery nudged them up to 118 all out. England then immediately fell to 3/50.

So this was not a flat pitch, and in Glenn McGrath, Shane Warne and Jason Gillespie, Australia had the rudiments of an okay-ish attack. Yet at this point Hussain combined with Graham Thorpe for a 288-run partnership – a development that, in terms of likelihood, probably ranked somewhere below the sudden arrival of the Spanish Inquisition for the majority of onlookers.

England laboured a bit while bowling Australia out a second time, but nevertheless secured a nine-wicket win.

Despite being far from intimately acquainted with such a scenario, even 1990s England were aware of the old saw that you should never change a winning team. Drunk on their success, they duly picked the same side for the second Test.

Nothing remarkable in that, you may think – but this was in fact the first time they had fielded an unchanged XI in home Tests, against any nation, since June 1991.

For six years and 32 Tests, England had fiddled and finessed, gambled and guessed, and basically plucked names out of a hat. Now, finally, they had hit upon a team they were happy with – a team that could go toe-to-toe with not just any old opponents, but Australia, their most bitter rivals.

Alas, 42.3 overs into this bold new era, they were all out for 77.

While the bad weather that had paradoxically stretched that rapid collapse into a third day ultimately saved them from defeat, the lesson was clear. Consistency might have been a policy that worked for Australia, but it clearly didn't for England. They resolved to never again make the

'Our chief weapons are fear, surprise and a Nasser double-century.'

bone-headed mistake of picking the same XI twice.

Team management duly fired up their merry-go-round and returned all names to the briefly snubbed selectorial hat – plus a few new ones, by way of apology for losing faith in headgear as a Test selection methodology.

It was back to shuffling the pack.[1] And, man, did they know how to shuffle. By the fifth Test of the series, they were making four changes. By the sixth, four more. But only by looking at the detail can we appreciate the full extent of the devilry.

For example, the fourth Test saw Mike Smith make his debut, replacing Andy Caddick. The fifth Test then saw the return of Caddick with Smith's debut now doubling up as his final Test.

Caddick's return coincided with the arrival of not one but two Hollioakes – both making their debuts. At one point, this resulted in a delightful passage of play where Adam and Ben Hollioake bowled in tandem to Mark and Steve Waugh. Whole nations' worth of cricketers to choose from, and the Ashes had essentially descended into a game of backyard cricket between two families.

England concluded that this was all a bit much and resolved to drop at least one Hollioake for the sixth and final Test. Australia, strangely, were rather less perturbed and retained both Waughs for roughly another five years. Adam (45 and 2, 0/24 and 2/21) was deemed to have outperformed Ben (28 and 2, 1/57 and 1/26) and so retained his place.

Meanwhile, at the top of the order, Mark Butcher, who had made his debut in the first Test, was dropped after the fourth, despite having made a couple of fifties. His omission meant Alec Stewart opened the batting as well as keeping wicket, despite having registered zero fifties in the series himself, while John Crawley (two fifties) vaulted up to three from six.

One Test later, Crawley was out, Butcher was in again and Stewart – an encouraging 87 now under his belt – was moved down to three.

But this isn't to say that throwing all the pieces in the air and seeing where they landed guaranteed failure. After

---

1 It seems wholly appropriate to cycle through erratic selection metaphors as rapidly as England were cycling through cricketers.

five Tests and eight wickets, England also saw fit to replace Robert Croft with Phil Tufnell. The latter promptly rewarded the selectors' whimsical, momentary faith in him by taking 11 wickets and winning the final Test.

That inexplicably narrow final series score of 3–2 to Australia was not, alas, sufficient to erase the memory of Shane Warne's celebratory 'stump dancing' on a Trent Bridge balcony a Test earlier. Hips sliding one way as the stump above his head slid the opposite way, this timeless jig – unleashed to celebrate Australia's retention of the Ashes – must go down as one of the sport's most iconic moments.

Why does it remain such a memorable event? Perhaps because it is so rare to get a single moment that seems to so perfectly capture the very essence of a particular human being. Bold, misguided and underpinned by complete immunity to embarrassment, to this day this rhythmic goading of England fans seems to encapsulate off-field Warne, in much the same way as the Gatting ball so perfectly sums up his on-field impact.

While the pain of being subjected to this sordid samba may never abate, the scars England sustained from picking the same XI twice healed rather more quickly. A year later, they would risk doing so again, beating South Africa in both matches. Strikingly, these were the first and second Tests played by Andrew Flintoff – a man who may yet earn himself another mention in this book ...

ACTIVITY CORNER

Gather together multiple ways of randomly selecting an England cricket team of the 1990s (pulling names out of a hat, shuffling a deck of cricket cards, consulting with your esteemed colleagues in the selection panel, et cetera). Now, if you were asked to randomly select which of those random selection methods you'd employ, using a different source of randomness (coin toss, rolling a die, online social media poll), how quickly would you become confused?

20

STEVE SMITH REVIEWS AND WALKS FOR AN LBW

AKA REVENGE OF THE SMITH

The 2019 Ashes saw Steve Smith strike his richest vein of ridiculous form in his entire career. So much so that we could have filled roughly one-third of this book with his antics during that series, had we not been contractually required to put in a bit more effort.

Smith also struck one of his richest veins of batting form in his entire career during the series. So much so that he seriously challenged one of Bradman's most famous records: most runs in a Test series (974 in the 1930 Ashes). Smith scored 774 runs in the 2019 Ashes at 110.57, despite playing one and a half Tests fewer than the Don. Could he have amassed another couple of hundred runs if given three more innings? You wouldn't have bet against it – which is utterly mad.

The pure batting form is even *more* ridiculous when one considers that this was Smith's return series after a year-long suspension, a fact he was reminded of at every turn by braying England fans waving sandpaper at him. In the face of such taunting, a normal human might be expected to wither at least a little. (Or even a not-at-all-normal human. David Warner, for example, tormented mercilessly by Stuart Broad around the wicket, scored 95 runs across the series at 9.50, which felt more like it. Even Warner's one decent score of 61 was somehow spent playing and missing at pretty much everything.)

Not Smith, though. He scored twin centuries (144 and 142) in the first Test, at Edgbaston. This included, in the first innings, adding 162 for the last two wickets with Peter Siddle and Nathan Lyon to rescue Australia from 8/122. He spent a little over eleven hours at the crease in that match, his constant presence ridiculous in itself.

As if in some kind of misheard Hotel California, Smith could be not out any time he liked, but he would always leave. And not just leave, but ridiculously leave. For this was the era of peak silly Steve Smith leaves, his prancing whack-a-mole refusal to play the ball executed with more energy than most batters put into hitting the bloody thing. To put that much effort into not doing something showed a level of ridiculousness that was truly elite (to use the popular jargon of the time).

Smith was also Australia's first-innings saviour in the second Test, at Lord's, and needed all his leaving prowess, dodging and weaving as debutant speedster Jofra Archer targeted him. In the first Test, Smith had successfully negotiated a Moeen Ali beamer, but, frankly, that wasn't much preparation for Archer's spell.

You can't bowl beach balls there to Steve Smith.

For Archer, conjuring a frightening absurdity of his own, defied the very concept of fatigue. Despite having already bowled 22 overs of high-quality fast bowling in the high 140-kilometres-per-hour range, he decided in the 23rd over that it was time to really ramp things up, hitting his fastest speeds of the Test. He burst past 150 kilometres per hour, hitting Smith on the arm and, eventually, the neck, forcing him to retire hurt on 80.

But if England thought knocking Smith out would make him any less absurd, they were sorely mistaken. When Siddle was caught behind, Smith returned to the crease to a soundtrack of respectful boos. He hit three fours in seven balls, and then, in a gag that paid off three innings' worth of setup, left a straight one that hit his pads in front of middle stump.

Mad enough for most batters. Nowhere near mad enough for 2019-era Smith. He immediately upped the absurdity of the moment one notch by walking. Then upped it several zillion notches by reviewing the decision *as he walked*.

Absolute top-tier nonsense.

Smith missed the second half of the second Test and the whole of the third with concussion, but such was the power of the walking-plumb-LBW review that it inspired others to follow his lead.

Marnus Labuschagne became the first concussion substitute in Test history, and picked up where Smith left off, being immediately knocked off his feet by a Jofra Archer short ball before top-scoring in Australia's three Smithless innings. Archer himself followed Smith's lead in the third Test, at Headingley (which was otherwise dominated by Ben Stokes offering his own brand of absurd cricket – stay tuned), by performing his own walking review.

In Archer's case, he ducked under a Pat Cummins bouncer but left his bat above his head, the ball hitting its full face on the way through to keeper Tim Paine. Archer, the ninth wicket to fall, reviewed and walked, and was safely off the ground by the time the third umpire reached his verdict.

With the Fort of Absurdity having been held by Labuschagne, Archer and Stokes, Smith returned for the fourth Test, at Old Trafford, and made up for lost ridiculous time. A beach ball blew onto the ground and Smith smacked it for four. He complained about glare from a broadcast van and had the umpires running off to put a towel on it. He brought up a fifty with a lunging leap at a ball outside off stump, where he seemed to only belatedly remember that he should hit it with his bat. He periscope-blocked an Archer short ball with a vertical bat above his head. He scored a century, then was caught by Stokes at slip off a Jack Leach no ball, and then made the century a double.

That was all in one innings. In his second innings that match, his first two scoring strokes were a) a ball he left that somehow still hit his bat and flew through cover for two, and b) four overthrows when he sent back a quick single-craving Travis Head. Smith was a batter in such good and ridiculous form that he tried to play two dot balls and accidentally got six runs for them. He added only 76 more, however, caught by Stokes at slip off a Jack Leach non-no-ball for 82, his lowest score of the series to that point.

In the fifth Test, Smith set a new personal low, scoring just 80 in the first innings, a failure he blamed on the flu. It felt a very *War of the Worlds*–like explanation. A strange, alien creature crashing down on England soil, wreaking unstoppable havoc, impervious to pretty much anything the English can throw at him – even bouncing back, scarier than ever, after a missile hits him directly in the head – and then finally undone by a simple flu virus.

In the final innings of the series, Smith was out for just 23, and we can therefore only assume that he was more Sudafed than man at that point.

But his work was done. A colossal batting effort from one of cricket's greatest ever – and, more importantly, a masterclass of nonsense from one of Australia's silliest batters. The kind of ridiculous series that Bradman could only dream of having. ('Oooh, I scored a duck in my last innings!' Do better, Donald.)

19

SARAH TAYLOR'S SLIP FIELDING

AKA KEEPING AT ARM'S LENGTH

This is the story of a batter reverse-sweeping a ball from outside off and getting caught at second slip. Nothing particularly unusual about any of that, except for the fact that there was no second slip. Or indeed any slips at all.

You may have a few questions at this point, but let's talk about a completely different ball first. This one was bowled by England's Nat Sciver (-not-yet-Brunt) to Ellyse Perry in the 2019 Ashes and it was a pretty rank one that went down the leg side.

What was striking about it was that, because of Perry's position and opacity, wicketkeeper Sarah Taylor would have completely lost sight of the ball from the time it pitched until the moment it hit her gloves – a pretty key period for the taking of a cricket ball, really. That she snaffled it so cleanly would have been an astonishing piece of keeping in itself, except that, upon contact, hands and ball immediately reversed direction and made their way directly to the stumps to remove the bails.

Perry was stumped, and it felt like the bails had come off even while she was in the process of missing the ball – and this all somehow happened with Taylor essentially operating blind.

You might at this point say that it had to be seen to be believed – but that would be wholly inaccurate, as for most people seeing went hand in hand with disbelieving. Seeing the dismissal in slow motion was believing: it was a stumping that could not really be perceived without that technological aid.

Oh, and it was off a wide.

That last aspect was in fact nothing new. Taylor had by this point gone a long way towards single-handedly establishing the leg-side wide as the most lethal delivery in all of cricket. (Actually, it was more often two-handedly, thanks to her exceptional footwork.)

Amanda-Jade Wellington had previously fallen to a very similar stumping in the 2017/18 Ashes. That one happened so quickly that Taylor had already appealed to the square leg umpire by the time Wellington got her foot down. (That's leg-side take, stump removal and appeal in the same timespan as one missed nurdle-to-leg. Hand-speed-wise, that puts her somewhere between a Monte Carlo blackjack dealer and *Blazing Saddles*'s Waco Kid.)

Elsewhere in that series, Taylor stumped Perry from what should have been an off-side wide in the second ODI, having also stumped her in the first match.

Make no mistake, Sarah Taylor could stump with the best of them (so much so that scorecards to this day still use her initials as the official abbreviation for that mode of dismissal) – and she could catch pretty well too.

There's a great YouTube video of one of Taylor's wicketkeeping drills. Positioned behind the stumps (where else?), she has a catching practice mat in front of her, on a length, into which a coach whangs two balls simultaneously.

The thing with these catching mats is that they are designed to deflect the ball – or in this case balls – in unpredictable directions. That means that if you're on the receiving end, you only have from pitching until the ball reaches you to react.

So the mat is on a length, Taylor is within touching distance of the stumps and the balls are whanged in decently hard. One arrives just outside the top of off stump, the other maybe 75 centimetres wider and a touch lower. Taylor catches both, simultaneously – one in each hand.

When you're dealing with a wicketkeeper who can do double-duty, taking two catches at a time, you don't really want to edge a single ball anywhere near them. What you generally want to do, instead, is middle that ball to somewhere they are not.

Sensibly enough, this was precisely what Jodie Fields did in the 2013 Ashes. The ball was bowled just outside off stump, Fields reverse-swept it to where second slip could have been but wasn't … and yet Sarah Taylor still caught it.

This was, by any measure, an irregular outcome. Taylor shifted her weight to move to her right when she saw Fields shaping to reverse, then she began moving as she swung, dived and stretched after she'd made contact, and then clawed the ball in at full stretch.

The ball wasn't so much going past her as away from her, and yet she caught it one fully-outstretched-human's length wide of the stumps. This is not a thing you see too often when the wicketkeeper is standing up to those stumps, and even less frequently when the batter has middled the thing.

'I only realised how far I'd dived when I saw the pictures after the game,' Taylor later told Sky Sports. 'I've always thought that if the ball is on the stumps and a batsman shapes up to paddle or reverse it, then they're in trouble if they miss, so I can hedge my bets and try to get across and cut off the shot.'

Apparently, this wasn't even her first time. 'I'd done it once before in a game, actually – catching Beth

Morgan. It relies on pure reaction speed and this catch was definitely all in the moment.'

Imagine having to bat in front of Sarah Taylor. Just think about the sheer size of the danger zone behind you. Miss a leg-side wide and you might get stumped; whack it towards second slip and she'll catch you.

Just by way of garnish, after taking that magnificent catch to help restrict Australia to 4/203 off a rain-reduced 36 overs, Taylor went out to bat at number three and made 64 off 59 balls to help secure the win. Needless to say, she also made a stumping in the match, but it was only difficult and not miraculous and so barely warrants a mention.

Teammates congratulate Danielle Hazell for the dismissal of Jodie Fields, as if it was anything at all to do with her.

18

STEVE WAUGH BATS WITH ONE LEG

AKA THE BUTCHER AND THE CALF

Steve Waugh's Ashes touring squad of 2001 was a merciless contingent of cricketing automatons. Mark Taylor had finished up his tenure as Australian captain after the 1998/99 Ashes, handing over to the elder Waugh the best Test team in the world. (To save needless first name repetition in this piece, 'Waugh' will mean Steve throughout, unless we explicitly call out Mark or, improbably, Dean. Or, even more improbably, Evelyn.)

'Nowhere to go from here but down' might have been the thought process of a more pessimistic captain. Waugh instead took the glass half-full-of-great-cricketers approach and set his side the fresh goal of becoming one of the best Test teams in history.

And then, because Waugh was a single-minded bastard who tended to bend the cricketing universe to his unyielding will, that's exactly what they became.

Waugh had a fraught start to his Test captaincy. Australia drew an away series against the West Indies (and even then only after offering an out-of-form, returning-from-injury Shane Warne as a fourth Test blood sacrifice to the Sir Frank Worrell Trophy gods). They then lost in Sri Lanka – a defeat punctuated by a brutal collision between Waugh and Jason Gillespie that broke the former's nose and the latter's leg.

After that, however, Waugh's team went on a record sixteen-Test winning streak. The side itself underwent some upgrades during that run. Ian Healy was swapped out for Adam Gilchrist. Matthew Hayden took the spot of Greg Blewett. Brett Lee emerged in place of Damien Fleming. And a subtle, beguiling version of Shane Warne took the place of the unsubtle, big-spinning version of his youth.

It was one hell of a cricket team.

Theoretically, they were a side that could still be beaten, but to do so required something remarkable. Just prior to the 2001 Ashes, India found something remarkable. Australia won the first Test by ten wickets, and sufficiently dominated the second Test to enforce the follow-on. Then VVS Laxman and Rahul Dravid put on a 376-run partnership. By pretty much any definition, this was a something upon which many onlookers remarked.

Harbhajan Singh proceeded to bowl like a wizard and India, somehow, recovered to win the series 2–1, sending the all-conquering, sixteen-match winning streak Australians into the Ashes on a two-match *losing* streak.

Naturally, they broke that streak immediately, thrashing England by an

Ever the image-conscious showman, Steve Waugh identifies and takes an opportunity to be the subject of an iconic photograph.

innings and 118 runs. In the second Test, England improved enough to make Australia bat a second time, but only barely, setting the visitors a fourth innings target of 14 (although, to England's credit, they took a couple of wickets in that mini-chase).

England improved still further in the third Test, taking *three* wickets in Australia's fourth-innings run chase of 158. Waugh didn't lose his wicket in the chase, but he did lose the use of his left calf, tearing it badly in two places while taking off for a quick single from the second ball he faced. The Australian captain received the call that his side had won the Ashes while in a wheelchair in hospital. Presumably this was not how he'd envisioned the moment.

Waugh's last Test act on England soil therefore looked certain to be being carried off on a stretcher to warm, thank-God-that's-the-last-we'll-see-of-you applause.

He, of course, had other ideas. Despite being told that his prognosis was a three-to-six-month lay-off, Waugh targeted the fifth Test for his return. (This was not three to six months away.)

In the meantime, Gilchrist captained Australia in the fourth Test, at Headingley, and for four days seemed to keep the Australian cricket machine humming smoothly in Waugh's absence.

With rain washing out entire sessions of play and threatening Australia's dreams of a clean sweep, Gilchrist declared just before the end of the fourth day, setting England 315 to win. More than enough time and runs for Australia to take a 4–0 lead, surely, assuming the rain held off.

The rain did hold off, but Mark Butcher didn't. Instead, England's number three – who wouldn't have been playing in the series at all, had it not been for the home side's own run of injuries – reached deep inside the Something Remarkable Box and pulled out the innings of a lifetime. He scored 173 not out from 227 balls to guide England to a superb six-wicket win.

Gilchrist described Butcher's batting that day as 'one of the greatest Ashes Test innings of all time'. England captain Nasser Hussain declared the knock 'phenomenal'. 'I cannot remember a better innings,' was Alec Stewart's assessment. 'You won't see a better innings,' concurred Mike Atherton.

Butcher's dad, Alan, a Test cricketer himself, said it was the 'best innings [Mark] has ever played', and that the knock was 'the icing on the cake and the cherry on top'.

'Enough of this endless, and needlessly dessert-centric, praise,' seemed to be Waugh's assessment. England winning a Test match? Get out of here with that.

And so the Australian captain returned for the fifth Test, and that clown Gilchrist was demoted back to vice-captain, where he could do no further harm. Was Waugh's torn calf muscle healed? No, of course not. A trivial detail. Not worth thinking about.

The recall of Justin Langer for Michael Slater at the top of the order meant the visitors played what would later be considered the platonic ideal of Waugh's Australian team (Hayden, Langer, Ponting, Waugh, Waugh, Martyn, Gilchrist, Lee, Warne, Gillespie, McGrath). Obviously, then, they won by an innings and 25 runs, on the back of a first innings score of 4/641 (declared).

Langer made 102 (retired hurt after hooking a ball into his own head), Mark Waugh 120, Hayden, Ricky Ponting and Damien Martyn 60-something each.

And the injured Steve Waugh? 157 not out. A nonsense of an innings, that, 30 runs in, saw him twinge a glute in the injured leg. This was followed by another calf injury shortly after that left Waugh with no choice but to start slogging, twenty-two years before Glenn Maxwell perfected the art of the legless thrash.

Waugh's century was eventually brought up with a hesitating, hobbling, staggering, desperately dived single to mid-on. Ridiculously, he acknowledged the crowd's applause by raising his bat from a prone position, stretched out flat on the ground, covered in dust.

A sane cricketer would have retired hurt at that point. Job done. Point made.

Waugh's reaction? *Why throw it away now?* he asked himself. *Keep going.*

These are not the thoughts of a well man. Still, as a wiser one once said, 'No one is ever holy without suffering' (Evelyn Waugh, *Brideshead Revisited*).

ACTIVITY CORNER

1. Tear your calf muscle badly enough to require three to six months of rehab.

2. Time how long it takes you to recover. Is it more than nineteen days? If so, why? (Use basic arithmetic if necessary.)

17

WHEN STUART BROAD FAILED TO DISMISS EXTRAS AT TRENT BRIDGE

AKA GONE IN SIXTY RUNS

Michael Clarke was the first Australia batter to last more than nine minutes. The captain's was an effort that really stopped the rot: a five-run partnership with Shaun Marsh, followed by a six-run partnership with Adam Voges, before a colossal eight-run alliance with wicketkeeper Peter Nevill.

That third partnership – the sixth of the innings – was the first to make it into double-figures in terms of balls faced.

Clarke was eventually out to the first ball of the seventh over of the match for 10. He was Stuart Broad's fifth wicket of the innings, but it actually took the bowler a moment to realise this because his victims had fallen so quickly.

That pace did not relent. A few minutes later, Australia were 7/33. Not long after, 60 all out.

It's hard to convey just how rapidly and comprehensively Broad dismantled Australia on that first morning at Trent Bridge in 2015. He took them apart as if they were a giant Lego penis and grandma was coming over. The Ashes were alive when he began his spell and England's when he finished.

Broad's final figures of 8/15 were in fact greatly marred when Nathan Lyon hit one-seventh of Australia's boundaries off his penultimate delivery.

The number eleven edged behind next ball. As a measure of how things were going by that point, he was caught at fifth slip.

Australia's entire innings lasted just 94 minutes, which meant that by lunch on the first day, England were trailing by just 47 runs with ten wickets in hand.

'Hopefully, we get a big lead,' said Broad at the innings break. They secured a lead of 331. Broad alone outscored Australia's two highest scorers combined (Mitchell Johnson with 13 and Clarke with 10), making 24 not out – although extras had in fact contributed the greatest weight of runs for Australia with 14.

The tourists' efforts batting first in this series were not what you would call consistent. We'll ignore their first effort of 308 all out because it's dull and irrelevant to the point we're trying to make. But in the second Test, they reached 1/360 on the way to 8/566 – an effort that suggested a solid batting line-up that should have harboured no fears of the first morning of a Test. Yet the same men only just about made it beyond the lunch break on day one of the third match of the series, thanks to a fifty from Chris Rogers. The second-highest score in that innings ended up being Adam Voges's 16.

Scores of 136 all out and 60 all out quite understandably persuaded Alastair Cook that the 8/566 was a one-off, but when he won the toss in the fifth and final Test and invited Australia to bat, the tourists reverted to solidity, racking up 481 – eight times as many runs – and ultimately secured an innings victory.

That result betrayed the fact that England's batting in the series was not much less erratic than their opponents'. They were dismissed for 149 in their first innings, despite packing the side with batting to the extent that Moeen Ali came in at number eight. (He top-scored with 30.)

But that wasn't even their worst effort. In the second Test, on the same pitch where Australia had passed 500, they were all out for 103 and Broad top-scored with 25.

In any normal series, that would surely have been remembered as one of the all-time great Ashes collapses. Maybe Broad didn't want to be associated with such a thing, even as the standout performer. Perhaps that's why he took the new ball two Tests later and took his first five wickets in 19 balls.

For those watching the 60 all out unfold, it quickly became apparent that it was not a matter of whether Broad would dismiss batters – or even how. The only doubt was which slip fielders would take the catches.

Mitchell Starc was given six to choose from and opted for Joe Root, as did his fellow Mitchell, Johnson, and also Steve Smith. Rogers and Clarke opted for Cook; Voges and Lyon went for Stokes; while Marsh ploughed his own furrow as the only man to pick out Ian Bell. His score wasn't unique, though. He, Rogers and David Warner all made ducks.

The decision to post a sixth slip was most likely made when Voges fell. The West Australian might have felt he'd got the ball wide enough to survive when he scissored an edge in that direction, only for fifth slip Stokes to elicit a pantomime awestruck facial expression from Broad by somehow clawing the ball in from somewhere behind him.

Stokes celebrated the catch by inadvertently steamrolling Jonny Bairstow onto his arse when the short leg fielder tried to embrace him.

Watching the match back for a Sky Sports 'watchalong' in 2020, Broad said that the emotion of that moment was so great that he lost his run-up. 'I was stood at my mark forgetting whether I go off my left foot or right. It sounds ridiculous. Fortunately, I got it back in the next over.'

Fortunate indeed, because he only had four wickets at that point.

'I have memories of frustration of that day,' he recalled. 'I remember when I got Johnson or Starc out that it felt like they had got 70 each and it had been overs and overs.'

Johnson did indeed play the longest innings. It was all of 25 balls.

ACTIVITY CORNER

1. Embark on a challenging project, one that will most likely require at least a full day of work and that may in fact prove impossible for you to complete – certainly without significant assistance from friends. Perhaps concreting a driveway, tiling a bathroom, moving house, brokering a peace treaty or designing and building a prototype for a new type of innovative lightweight electric vehicle.

2. Completely finish it single-handedly within ninety-four minutes.

The face that launched a thousand memes.

16

STEVE HARMISON BOWLS A WIDE

AKA STARTING OVER AND STARTING OUT

Umpire Steve Bucknor employs both arms to state the bleeding obvious.

The 2005 Ashes was a series riddled with more key moments than a 1970s swingers party. The earliest such moment came from the second ball of the series, courtesy of England fast bowler Steve Harmison.

Harmison was a formidable six-foot-four behemoth. Justin Langer, facing him in the opening over, was very much not. But Langer was up for the fight, allowing the first delivery of the series to safely pass his off stump, before bouncing around the crease like an antsy boxer.

If this was a boxing match, however, it was one in which Harmison landed the first blow. Next ball, he hit a recoiling Langer on the elbow. Langer dropped his bat and walked away from the crease, as physio Errol Alcott ran on to examine the opener. (His diagnosis? 'You've been hit by a cricket ball, JL.')

The blow to Langer's arm was the first sign that England were not going to be the usual clown show that Australia had become accustomed to over the preceding sixteen years of Ashes cricket. Ricky Ponting's men were in a fight.

In case that point wasn't clear from the Langer blow, Harmison emphasised it further when Ponting arrived at the crease. Once again, it took only two balls for Harmison to hit the batter. This time he drew blood, cutting the Australian captain's cheek with a delivery too fast for his attempted pull shot. (Let's savour that for a bit: the ball was too fast for a *Ricky Ponting* pull shot. No surprise then that, at his peak, Harmison was the number one bowler in the world.)

Harmison's blows were a precursor to what was to come. A Steve Harbinger, if you will. The 2005 Ashes was to be a heavyweight battle for the ages.

In the return bout of 2006/07, Harmison again bowled the first over of the Ashes. Never mind hitting the batters this time, though. Instead, it took him two balls before he was even able to hit the cut strip, his first delivery infamously sailing wide to Andrew Flintoff at second slip.

Why wait for the second ball of the series to deliver a key moment when you can provide one from the very first ball?

Because the Harmison first-ball wide also foreshadowed what was to come. This series was not to be a heavyweight battle for the ages, despite all the (justifiable) hype leading into it. Instead, England had once again brought their clown show on tour, and, while it's always justifiable to beat up a clown, they're notoriously unlikely to fight back, what with their oversized shoes, their preference for throwing pies rather than punches, and their unhelpful tendency to slip on any ringside banana peels.

Harmison was hauled off after two overs, having conceded 17 runs (four boundaries to Langer, plus the wide). Australia went on to make 9/602 (declared). England responded with 157, and with a narrow lead of 445, Ponting opted to bat again, eventually setting England the small matter of 648 runs for victory.

England did not reach that victory target in this first Test. Nor did they reach a victory target in any of the four others, succumbing 5–0 in the first Ashes whitewash since 1920/21.

The Harmison wide that had so effectively set the tone became the gold standard for ridiculous first balls of an Ashes series. A towering feat of cricketing nonsense.

And then, fifteen years later, a contender for the crown arrived, in the distorted form of Rory Burns, who somehow contrived to be bowled behind his legs by Mitchell Starc from the first ball of the series.

We've already discussed the Burns dismissal, of course, back at No. 36 on this countdown. But now it's time to see which of these Gabba-delighting moments was the most ridiculous first ball in Ashes history.

Let's do this scientifically, scoring each of the deliveries on the key measures of surprise, impact on match result, English deflation, Australian commentator reaction and Gabba reaction.

SURPRISE

The Harmison wide was *very* surprising. Wides in Test cricket are unusual to begin with (and therefore extra-unusual to literally begin with).[1] And this wasn't any old wide – this was a wide to second slip. Proper unexpected gear. **9/10**

In contrast, Mitchell Starc seemingly takes wickets in his first over every other match he plays. It's kind of his thing. And the first ball is just the first part of the first over. Barely worth remarking upon, really. **3/10**

---

1 At the time of writing, the record for the greatest number of wides in a Test is 38. There have been over 400 Tests in which there have been more wickets than that. Wides are rarer than wickets, and hence more surprising.

IMPACT ON MATCH RESULT

Harmison's wide contributed one run to the 804 that Australia scored in the Test. **0.01243/10**

Burns's wicket was the first of 20 that Australia took in the Test. **0.5/10**

ENGLISH DEFLATION

As comical as the Harmison wide was, it didn't immediately deflate England's hopes of retaining the urn. Flintoff calmly gathered the ball at slip and everybody had a bit of a laugh. It was a foreboding moment only in retrospect – easily the least effective kind of foreboding. **2/10**

Burns's wicket, however, felt more immediately ominous. England had been unhappily stuck in Covid-19 quarantine in the lead-up to the series, with limited ability to prepare. Having your opening batter somehow fall across his stumps and get bowled behind his legs felt like precisely the kind of thing free-range England cricketers might have stamped out of their game. This was almost certainly the instant Stuart Broad decided he would declare this series void. **8/10**

AUSTRALIAN COMMENTATOR REACTION

(It's very difficult to find any historical record of the reaction from the various UK commentary teams. Mostly, one imagines, because these are not moments that most England fans want to lodge online for posterity.)

'Whoa! Wide delivery, taken at slip by the skipper,' said Bill Lawry when calling the Harmison delivery. 'The nerves are showing already.' Richie Benaud then followed up with some musings on nervousness. Measured stuff from a couple of veteran commentators. **5/10**

'And he's got him! Unbelievable!' was Tim Lane's commentary on Channel Seven, as Burns's stumps were splattered. Over on Triple M Radio, James Brayshaw's contribution to the moment was an unintelligible roar. On Fox Sports, meanwhile, Shane Warne – bless his blinkered memory – immediately insisted that Starc's delivery 'looked like a half-volley at leg stump that he missed'. A variety pack of nonsense responses. **8/10**

GABBA REACTION

It's the Gabba. Any England failure is always met with precisely the same level of cheering, chortling, delighted derision. **10/10** to both moments.

OVERALL SCORES

Harmison's wide:
26.01243 OUT OF 50

Burns's wicket:
29.5 OUT OF 50

So there you have it. The award for the 'Most Ridiculous First Ball of an Ashes Series' goes to … (opens envelope) Zak Crawley for 'Drilling Pat Cummins through cover for four'?

You get out of here, Zak. You're not *La La Land*-ing this. Heck, you're not even eligible in most of these scoring measures. Off you scoot, back to No. 48, where you belong.

15
90S 99S

**AKA THE BAWL
OF NO CENTURY**

When did the 1990s begin? Those among you with calendrical expertise will no doubt have a specific date in mind here, but England cricket fans have a very particular understanding of the 90s that doesn't exactly tally with convention.

As multiple entries in this book have already suggested, to talk about England cricket of the 1990s is to reference a somewhat longer span of time, during which the Test team was shaped by an institutional drive to get the absolute least out of the (very many) players who comprised it.

In terms of actual dates, it probably began with Australia's Ashes victory in 1989, finally drawing to a close in 2005. You could even make a case that it got underway in the fifth Test of the previous Ashes, because after England won the 1986 Boxing Day Test, it was another six years before they beat Australia again in a Test match.

You want to be more specific? Ooh, let's go for Ian Botham's golden duck in the second innings (dismissed by debutant Peter Taylor as part of his claim for the No. 44 spot in this countdown). That feels like an appropriately symbolic moment.

Now, 1987 to 2005 might sound like a very long and fun decade to an Australian, but it's important to note that, for the English, it felt way, way longer.

Even by traditional measures, the 1993 Ashes was right in the thick of the decade, but its England 1990s credentials were also almost immediately apparent.

In the first Test, Graham Gooch was the only England batter to pass 50 in either innings; Mike Gatting was on the receiving end of the Ball of the Century; and England lost by 179 runs. Just to really underline that this wasn't England's decade, Gooch was out handling the ball in the second innings, backhanding it away from the stumps before it could land on them.

So far, so harrowing, from England's perspective – but at least things couldn't get any worse. Except that this was the 1990s, so of course they could.

England hadn't beaten Australia at Lord's since 1934 and the tourists duly queued up to get themselves onto the honours board (which is a lot more by-the-book in its view on how far the 90s span). After Allan Border won the toss and elected to bat, the top three – Mark Taylor, Michael Slater and David Boon – all made it to three figures. Taylor (111) and Slater (152) put on

Mike Atherton almost immediately regrets this newfangled idea of 'crawling between the wickets'.

260 for the first wicket. Boon made 164 not out.

Australia's number four, Mark Waugh, comfortably and chancelessly made his way to 99, at which point he was bowled off his pad by Phil Tufnell.[1]

Oh.

It would – and really should – have been the first innings in Test history in which the top four batters all made centuries. Positively enraged by this failure, Border ordered Waugh to open the bowling by way of penance after he eventually declared Australia's innings on an eye-watering 4/632. (Dismissed for 77, Border was in fact himself Australia's least successful batter of the innings.)

The decision to give the new ball to Waugh was, admittedly, also influenced by the unavailability of Craig McDermott, who had been rushed to hospital with a twisted bowel. (Ouch!) This left Australia with a three-man attack and just the one seamer, Merv Hughes.

Given that each wicket in the match had thus far come at a cost of 158 runs, it didn't seem as if the game was likely to move on quickly. But 1990s England's self-destructive impulses weren't going to be suppressed by the small matter of Mark Waugh opening the bowling. They duly bundled themselves out for 205 – Robin Smith's 22 the second-highest score behind Mike Atherton's lone-hand 80.

Border looked at his three-man bowling attack, then looked at England and invited them to follow on.

That second innings was a little more successful (if 'successful' is really the appropriate word to use here – which it almost certainly isn't). Tim May and Shane Warne were just one ball away from having bowled 100 overs between them when the final wicket was taken to secure victory by an innings and 62 runs.

The most memorable moment of the match had long since passed by that point, however. It had come with Atherton and Mike Gatting batting nicely together with just one wicket down. The two had put on a century partnership when Atherton suddenly found himself flat on his face, halfway down the pitch, watching Ian Healy run him out for 99.

---

1   In the next Ashes series, facing the same bowler, Waugh decided it was a good time to attempt the reverse sweep for the first time in his career. Alas, he succeeded only in dragging a ball that would have passed well outside leg stump into it.

It was almost as if England had seen Waugh dismissed for 99 and brainstormed some one-upmanship. What could be more infuriating than getting out for 99? Getting run out for 99, of course! In fact, let's throw in a dash of slapstick and have someone run out for 99 while he's still on his hands and knees after slipping and falling on his arse.

Speaking to *The Cricketer* years later, Gatting gave his account of the incident: 'Mike [Atherton] hit it in front of square and Merv ran around. In Mike's mind there was three and he went like a train, but I was late leaving my end. There was no way I could get to the other end, so I said no. He went back, but slipped and then slipped again. I watched on in horror.'

So that sounds like Atherton was hell-bent on reaching his hundred and didn't make allowances for Mike Gatting being … well, Mike Gatting.

The only problem with Gatting's explanation of events is that there's footage of the incident, and it puts a different spin on things. When you watch it again, it's obvious that Atherton looked very uncertain about that third run and only set off because he saw Gatting coming. Turning for that attempted third run, Atherton grounded his bat, planted his feet and began to raise his hand to signal either 'no' or at the very least 'wait'.

But then something happened that compelled Atherton to set off running again. That something was, presumably, Mike Gatting saying 'yes'.

'Mike Gatting called me for the run that would have brought up my 100, then sent me back,' recalled Atherton. 'I slipped and was yards short when Ian Healy broke the stumps. I was desperate to get a century, to get on the Lord's honours board and desperate to help England save a Test.'

Together with his first innings 80, the knock did at least secure Atherton's place in the side. Indeed, two Tests later he was made captain and immediately led England to victory at The Oval – their first win against Australia in eighteen matches, running all the way back to that 1986 Boxing Day Test.

He never did make it onto that Lord's honours board, though, cruel numerical stickler that it is.

As for Waugh, he made it there a little later in the 1990s when he was run out for 108 in the 2001 Ashes.

14

ASHTON AGAR DOES SOMETHING UNEXPECTED

AKA AA BATTERY

Ashton on his way to falling two runs – and two letters – short of an Ashes ton.

When James Pattinson was out LBW to Graeme Swann in the first Test of the 2013 Ashes to have Australia 9/117, fans back home nodded in grim acceptance.

'Yes, this feels about right,' was the general vibe among supporters. Ever since the previous Ashes series, which had ended with England securing three innings victories and performing a celebratory sprinkler dance on the MCG after retaining the urn, Australian cricket fans had seen their hope whittled away. All that remained was a vague but pervasive air of 'I'm not mad, just disappointed'.

In the most recent summer, Australia had been beaten by South Africa at home, then been thrashed 4–0 on a tour of India, which had descended into intra-team acrimony amid a scandal that saw four players suspended for a Test for not doing their homework.

During a warm-up for the Champions Trophy in England just before the Ashes, Australia had responded to India's 6/308 off their 50 overs by being bowled out for 65.

A little embarrassing, yes, you might be thinking. But just a warm-up game. Let's not panic until we see how the tournament unfolded. Ah … knocked out in the group stage without a single win, having lost to England and Sri Lanka and had a match against New Zealand rained off.

That's a shame. But at least, after the game against England, nobody punched Joe Root in a) the head or b) a Birmingham nightclub, right? *Right?*

Wrong, of course. For David Warner received a (first) suspension from the Australian cricket team for striking precisely such a blow. (His full-time stand-in ODI captain, George Bailey, suggested that Warner had taken the disciplinary decision 'on the chin', which seemed fitting.)

With on-field and off-field crises enveloping the side, coach Mickey Arthur had his work cut out for him to bring the team together in time for the Ashes. Even more so when Cricket Australia had his work cut out *from* him two weeks before the series began, sacking him in favour of Darren Lehmann.

The Australian cricket team were not so much lulling England into a false sense of security, as LOLZing them into a genuine one.

Lehmann didn't have time to accomplish much leading into the first Test, and mostly limited himself to making selectorial tweaks to the side that had succumbed to India.

ASHTON AGAR DOES SOMETHING UNEXPECTED

Chris Rogers came in to replace the suspended Warner. Captain Michael Clarke returned, taking the place of Glenn Maxwell, who hadn't made the squad. Vice-captain Brad Haddin regained the wicketkeeping spot ahead of Matthew Wade. A one-to-one fast-left-arm-Mitchell replacement saw Starc in for Johnson.

Oh, and Nathan Lyon, who had taken 7/94 and 2/71 in Australia's most recent Test, was dropped in favour of a teenager of whom pretty much nobody had heard.[1] That teenager – Ashton Agar – was the man walking in at number eleven to replace Pattinson in the first Test.

It was drinks on the first morning of the second day. Australia were still 98 runs behind England's first-innings score of 215, and the hapless Australian side was performing as expected. The next few hours brought pretty much the least expected thing you're ever likely to see on a cricket ground.

For an hour, Agar launched a carefree counterattack against England's short-ball bowling, hitting seven fours and a six to race past Warwick Armstrong's 111-year-old record of 45 not out for the highest score by a number eleven batter on debut.

It was now 10pm on the east coast of Australia. Under ordinary circumstances, this would be lunch. A forty-minute break that separates the 'just about time for bed' casuals from the 'let's kick on for a bit' tragics.

But these weren't ordinary circumstances. Australia were (still) nine wickets down, and so England were given up to an extra half-hour to end the innings.[2]

Instead, Australia used it as an opportunity for thirty minutes of further run-plundering. Phillip Hughes, only a couple of years older than Agar, and batting at six for the first time in a career mostly spent as an opener, had been faced with the novel challenge of batting with

---

1   A potentially crisis-inducing selection decision, because Lyon was the keeper of the team song, so if Australia won the Test, it was unclear who would sing the song. Fortunately, this proved not to be a problem.
2   Astonishingly, in the fourth innings of the Test, England were again given an extra half-hour with Australia nine wickets down. And, again, failed to take the wicket, sending everybody to lunch on the final day with either 20 runs or one wicket needed for victory. In that second innings, Pattinson was batting at number eleven and scored 25 not out in a tenth-wicket partnership of 65. Australia batted all the way down to number eleven in this Test. The problem was that they didn't bat all the way up to number one.

the tail. Instead of farming the strike, he decided to go with the exact opposite approach. Spraying the strike with weedkiller? Salting the earth of the strike? Rezoning the strike as a residential area, preparing it for new housing developments that make home ownership affordable for hardworking families in the local community?

Whatever you call it, that was what Hughes did, passing the strike to Agar at every opportunity. Agar accepted the strike and swiftly brought up a run-a-ball half-century. He took to Swann, lofting him down the ground for a second six, then hitting him for a pair of fours to go past Glenn McGrath's highest score by an Australian number eleven (61).

Hughes then joined in the fun, hitting Stuart Broad for three fours in an over to bring up the century partnership and give Australia the lead. The pair went to late-lunch at 9/229, 14 runs ahead, and only the maddest or most exhausted of Australian cricket fans were going to bed.

Social media was abuzz. Another one-Test Australian bowler who'd performed extraordinary feats with the bat on debut joined in the excitement. 'He keeps smashing Agar bombs!!' tweeted a young, injured and future foreword-penning Pat Cummins.

After the break, the Agar bombs continued to be smashed. Two fours off Broad's first over after lunch gave Hughes and Agar the record for Australia's highest ever tenth-wicket partnership. Four overs later, they had the highest for all nations, and Agar was into the 90s.

When he reached 96, he had the highest ever score by a number eleven, surpassing Tino Best's 95 against England just a year earlier. And then, two runs later, he was out, caught in the deep by Swann off the bowling of Broad, for a stunning 98 from 101 balls.

The reaction of the Australian fans at the ground was epitomised by Agar's mother, who leapt from her seat in excitement at the initial shot, thinking he'd brought up his century with it. She then clutched her hands to her chest as she saw Swann circling beneath the ball, before slumping back down, head bowed in disappointment at the loss of his wicket.

In commentary, Ian Botham described it as a 'fine, fine catch', before adding, 'How unlucky is that for the young man?' He immediately followed with: 'I wish he had got the hundred.'

Agar's teammates in the dressing room for once agreed with Beefy, also reacting with visible dismay to him missing out on the ton. Steve Smith, hands half-covering his eyes, stared blankly into space via the remaining eye-halves. Shane Watson, standing behind him, exhaled in disappointment and turned away, unwilling to watch Swann's celebration of the wicket. Lehmann offered a thin-lipped, eyebrows-raised mask of disbelief.

Everybody back in Australia was similarly crestfallen. Heck, surely even all but the most parochial of England supporters felt for him, as evidenced by the crowd rising as one to applaud him from the ground.

Agar's reaction to this gut-wrenching tragedy? A hey-ho, 'these things happen' smiling shrug.

13

A RUN-OUT STEALS THE SHOW

AKA RICKY PONTING'S PRATTFALL

A phlegmatic and philosophical Ricky Ponting accepts his run-out fate with impeccable grace.

It's instructive to think through all the significant contributors to the 2005 Trent Bridge Test and consider how, in almost any other game, any one of them would have delivered the most memorable moment of the match.

First of all, Shaun Tait made his Test debut. Truly fast bowlers don't come around too often, so this felt like a big deal when it was announced at the toss. But while Tait was swift, his overshadowing was even swifter as Andrew Flintoff hit a hundred in the first innings.

Flintoff was an extremely popular cricketer among England fans, and after his efforts at Edgbaston and Old Trafford his status was probably at its absolute zenith. This acclaim was not, however, born of reliable run-scoring. His Trent Bridge effort was only his fifth Test hundred and the novelty only made the innings feel more significant.[1]

That innings constituted pretty high-level entertainment from an England fan's perspective, but even that excitement was short-lived, because after Flintoff's efforts got the home team to 477, Matthew Hoggard and Simon Jones took England a good few paces towards a series lead by reducing Australia to 5/99 by the close of the second day.

Jones had already delivered one should-have-been-memorable moment when the ball hit his stumps without removing a bail while he'd been batting. His 5/44 was rather more significant in terms of the match, though.

The Australia innings also featured Andrew Strauss's 'Superman' catch, diving full length to his left to snaffle Adam Gilchrist off the bowling of Flintoff – a catch so astonishing the entire crowd gasped as one when the replay was shown in the ground. This incredible take more than made up for Strauss's comedy first-innings dismissal, when he'd managed to sweep the ball into his own foot and from there to Matthew Hayden at slip.

After that, it was Michael Vaughan's turn. When he invited[2] Australia to bat again, it was the first time they had followed on in seventeen years and 190 Tests.

---

1 Hindsight later revised this to 'fifth and final Test hundred' in a post-hoc underlining of its rarity.
2 As always, an invitation that the invitee is not able to decline, which does tend to render it less inviting. (See also Christmas dinner with [insert name of awful family relation].)

Rather sadly, that second Australia innings featured Jones's final over in Test cricket, as he succumbed to an ankle injury from which he would never return. His absence from the bowling attack for all but four overs allowed Australia to reach 387, setting England a seemingly manageable 129 to win.

Enter Shane Warne.

Rarely a monochrome cricketer, Warne was having a colourful match even by his standards. After carrying the Australia attack with 4/102 in England's first innings, he had notched a golden duck (to Jones) in his first knock before slashing 45 off 42 balls in his second. After his fifth over in England's second innings, he had figures of 3/7 to his name, having accounted for the entire top order. His fourth wicket – England's seventh – with the score on 116, was Geraint Jones.

Thirteen runs may not sound too far from victory, but it was 13 runs that now needed to be scored with Matthew Hoggard at the crease. There was also the small matter of Brett Lee screaming in at top pace[3] and Shane Warne bowling like only Shane Warne ever

has. In those circumstances, 13 was in fact an incredibly large number of runs. The easiest way to comprehend this was to look at the demeanour of the next man in, Steve Harmison, who appeared to be all but chewing through his bat handle with nervousness on the balcony. The old cricketing saw that 'one wicket brings two' has rarely, if ever, seemed such an absolute nailed-on certainty.

Hoggard had, at this point in his career, tried to carve a niche for himself as a specialist nightwatcher. This generally involved repeated deployment of his solitary stroke, which was the forward defensive. When the Yorkshireman unexpectedly creamed Lee to the off-side boundary with just a handful of runs to get, it was another moment that would ordinarily have qualified as unforgettable.

Shortly afterwards, Ashley Giles hit the winning runs. These were two of England's most loyal and workmanlike performers. To see them have their day in the sun – with bats in hand, no less – might well have provided the defining image of the match.

These tail-end titans were, however,

---

3   'Who is this Shaun Tait you speak of?'

up against not just a fifth of Flintoff's hundreds, but also Simon's swing, Superman Strauss, Vaughan, Warne and the dawn of Shaun – a veritable cornucopia of champagne moments, any one of which could have qualified as the most memorable of the match. In any other game, perhaps they would have. But not in this one – because Ricky Ponting had got himself run out, hadn't he?

When you talk about Trent Bridge 2005, that's the moment everyone remembers. The score was 2/155 in Australia's second innings. Damien Martyn played Flintoff into the off side, Martyn and Ponting decided there was a run, and substitute fielder Gary Pratt threw the stumps down.

Run-outs happen and substitute fielders are rarely incompetent. So what?

The thing is, throughout the 2005 Ashes, England's fast bowlers had been on and off the field frequently,[4] so Ponting was, shall we say, a little displeased about the specific nature of his dismissal.

The reason why this moment remains so especially memorable is because Ponting utilised his long walk back to the changing rooms to verbally expectorate every last drop of that displeasure.

'A bit of carry-on from me,' was how Ponting put it himself, when graciously invited to relive the moment by the Lord's Cricket Ground YouTube channel some years later.

Ponting chiefly expressed his displeasure by having 'a few choice words' with England coach Duncan Fletcher, who had taken the opportunity to emerge on the England balcony, where for some reason he saw fit to deploy the almost-never-seen Fletcher smile. (Something of which he was, apparently, capable. 'All my family have low jowls; just a slight lifting of them creates a smile,' he explained in his autobiography.)

The TV coverage captured Ponting storming through the crowd on his way back to the Australian dressing room, gazing upwards at Fletcher, giving full voice to his heartfelt opinions on matters pertaining to the manner of his dismissal.

Fletcher, unseen, just grinned. 'I smiled at Ricky Ponting. He didn't smile back. He was in a terrible temper for some reason,' Fletcher later wrote.

---

4   One might even say gleefully, antagonistically frequently.

'Quite why he was blaming me when his partner, Damien Martyn, had called him for a suicidal single to cover, I don't know.'

The finer points of Ponting's case were apparently unsuccessfully conveyed, but Fletcher felt that he got the gist. 'I do not honestly know what he was saying, but it did not appear very friendly. I think that we can safely assume he was abusing me.'

While it was widely acknowledged that England's fast bowlers hadn't always satisfactorily justified their temporary absences from the field during play, on this occasion there could be no complaints – not unless Simon Jones's career-long susceptibility to injury and failure to return to Test cricket ever again were nothing more than a painstakingly established long-term cover story to conceal the ruse.

12

AUSTRALIA'S OPENERS ARE RUN OUT (× 6)

AKA GWOOD GRIEF!

Opening batters have a unique position in a cricket side. They are the only pair in the XI who know for certain that they will bat together, marching middleward at the start of the team's innings to face the new ball. (Well, mostly – more on this shortly.)

Because of this, openers tend to develop a bond, as anybody who failed to avert their eyes from the tens of thousands of Matthew Hayden–Justin Langer century partnership celebrations can attest.

Obviously, not all opening partnership bonds reach the emotional heights of Hayden and Langer. But what one expects, at a bare minimum, given the unique nature of their joint role, is a better-than-average understanding of the basics of batting together. You wouldn't, for example, expect to see the openers being run out in every single Test of a series.

Comedy cricket–loving reader, we give you the Australian openers of the 1978/79 Ashes.

Australia went into this series shorn of their first-choice XI. Also most of their second-choice XI. Probably a couple of third-choicers too. Kerry Packer had seen to that, signing up Dennis Lillee, Jeff Thomson, Rod Marsh, David Hookes, Doug Walters, more Chappells than you can possibly count[1] and many, many others for his World Series Cricket circus. (Sadly, not a literal circus. Len Pascoe as a lion tamer! Magnificent Rick McCosker on the flying trapeze! Ashley Mallett, human cannonball! Don't tell me you don't want to see that.)

Of course, Packer had purloined a few players from England, too. But it was only a handful, which meant that Mike Brearley led a squad that still contained the likes of Ian Botham, Geoff Boycott, David Gower, Derek Randall, Graham Gooch and Bob Willis. More than enough firepower to effortlessly account for Graham Yallop's weakened Australians. (To be fair to England, they'd arrived at the Gabba as holders of the Ashes, having beaten a full-strength Australian side 3–0 in 1977. It wasn't solely a case of them pwning the n00bs.)

So Australia couldn't entertain their home crowds by beating England. But they could entertain in other ways. And since it remains a cricketing fact that the run-out is the form of dismissal that is most inherently comic,

---

1 Assuming you can't count to three.

A rare photo of Graeme Wood making his ground.

Graeme Wood and his opening co-conspirators, Gary Cosier (first Test), Andrew Hilditch (sixth Test) and Rick Darling (the other Tests) went to work.

In the first Test at the Gabba, Wood and Cosier opened the batting together for the first time. On the fourth ball of the Test, just as commentator Frank Tyson praised the pair as both being 'very good runners between the wickets', they took a sharp single to Gower, who underarmed the ball into the stumps with Cosier short of his ground. This, perhaps not coincidentally, was also the last Test where Wood and Cosier opened together.

The second Test saw Darling join Wood at the top of the order. Technically speaking, this new partnership didn't end with a run-out. Wood was already out (and so were Kim Hughes and Yallop) when Peter Toohey belatedly sent Darling back after he tried to sneak a single on a close-in misfield.

Nevertheless, it was still an opener being run out. And in the third Test, Wood and Darling gave us the more comically satisfying version of the opener being run out when Wood aborted an attempted single hit straight to mid-on, stranding Darling halfway down the pitch. In the fourth Test, it was Wood's turn to be run out. This time it was Darling already out, so Wood had to make do with ending up at the same end as Hughes, discussing the merits (or otherwise) of a single as the stumps at the other end were broken.

The fifth Test? Another Hughes/Wood combo, with Wood succumbing to a Boycott direct hit from mid-on. The sixth Test saw Darling, struck during the fifth Test by a Bob Willis short ball that had caused him to black out, replaced by debutant Andrew Hilditch. Wood successfully ran the newcomer out for just 3.

Yet despite Wood and Co.'s entertainingly shoddy running between the wickets, crowds for the 1978/79 Ashes continued to plummet. By the sixth Test, Australian cricket fans' legendary contempt for a losing side saw attendances drop to what Wisden called 'alarming levels'.

With England's openers unwilling to join in the run-out fun, Australia resorted to even more unorthodox tactics in the final innings of the series. Defending just 34 in the fourth innings on a classic turning SCG pitch, Yallop opened the bowling with two spinners, Bruce Yardley and Jim Higgs.

A bit rough to expect a pair of spinners to take the new ball, you might be thinking. In which case, you are of a like mind with Yallop, who thought not just outside the box, but outside the entire cricketing protective kit, by taking the *old* ball instead. The 103-over-old ball they'd used in England's first innings.

Brearley, who was not just England's captain but also one of their unfunny openers, objected to this brazen reimagining of the sport, but to no avail. The home-town umpires decreed the use of the old ball to be 'fair enough!' and, one imagines, taunted the England captain for carrying on about it. 'You're only chasing 34 runs,' they presumably told him. 'Live a little.'

While Brearley headed out to bat, England's team manager, Doug 'The Stickler' Insole, tediously checked the Laws of Cricket. By the time he reached the fifth of those laws, he confirmed the suspicions of Brearley and everybody else who'd previously seen the sport of cricket played. Yallop's old-ball shenanigans were not, technically speaking, legal.

With England already closing in on the target, though, Insole let the matter slide. Australia's spinners pounced on this moment of weakness, dismissing Boycott still three runs short of victory. The wicket brought Randall to the crease, where he was startled by the sight of a snake on the pitch! Although, as it turned out, just a plastic snake placed there by an irredeemable Australian wag. Brearley, having had enough of the increasingly ludicrous Australian nonsense, then hit a four to end the Test.

England had won the series 5–1, but they'd been rather sadly caught taking their cricket a little too seriously. Had their openers run themselves out at every opportunity? Had their captain made up new rules for the sport on a whim? Had any of them amusingly terrified their opponents with facsimiles of famously lethal wildlife?

No, no and no. And they left Australian shores the poorer for it. Enjoy your urn, lads.

ACTIVITY CORNER

Pretend you are a captain of an international cricket side. Make a list of five Laws of Cricket you'd like to change to benefit your team. Rank them in order of how partisan the home umpires would have to be to allow you to get away with this.

11

ENGLAND'S HEAD START

AKA BOXING MIS-MATCH

James Anderson foolishly fritters away another of England's small and diminishing stockpile of successful moments Down Under.

Sometimes the first day of a Test match ends and the TV anchor proclaims the game – and perhaps also the series – 'perfectly poised'. More often, one team has had a good day and the other a bad day, at which point whoever's trying and failing to be Richie Benaud that day tends to point out that 'there's plenty still to play for' or something along those lines. Team A 'will be looking to fight back on day two', 'put together a few partnerships' or 'take early wickets' – that kind of thing. You know the drill.

It's rare, but occasionally the first day's play is so hopelessly one-sided that, when it ends, our host can only conclude: 'Well, that's pretty much that. Let's have a look what's coming up over the rest of the summer.'

When England are touring Australia, that last one occurs not entirely infrequently, but it happens in England's favour basically never. Or at least that's what everyone thought until day one of the 2010 Boxing Day Test.

The 2010/11 Ashes is now largely remembered for the bizarre mincing operation carried out by the tourists, which saw Australia's bowlers painfully ground into a hideous paste by Alastair Cook, Jonathan Trott et al. (see No. 29). But that wasn't how it seemed at the time. Shorn of hindsight, the fourth Test in particular arrived with a sense of normal service having resumed.

To quickly recap, England held the Ashes after triumphing 2–1 in 2009. They had then opened their defence in traditional fashion by ceding a 221-run first-innings lead at the Gabba. At this point they'd made 1/517 in their second innings and everyone had been very confused.

While the first Test ended in a draw, England's run-scoring freakishness spilled over into the second Test at Adelaide, where they racked up 5/620 – enough to secure an innings victory.

Australia weren't batting dreadfully, though: 481 and 1/107 in the first Test; 245 and 304 in the second. They then won at the WACA after notching similar scores to the second Test, in so doing achieving their dual goals of levelling the series and reminding England that they weren't actually supposed to win Test matches in Australia.

Day one of the fourth Test therefore shaped up as a mouth-watering prospect for Australians in particular: Boxing Day at the MCG in front of 90,000 people, their team coming into form, the Ashes up for grabs. What a prospect!

There was significantly less enthusiasm at the start of day two, which England effectively began with an innings-and-59-run head start.

Even for those in the Northern Hemisphere who didn't directly follow proceedings, day one was a jarring chunk of Test cricket. Time differences being what they are, many Britons saw the close-of-play score first thing in the morning on Boxing Day – a strong contender for the bleariest, most brain-scrambled hour of the year. It therefore took a while for most people to recognise that that year's greatest Christmas present had arrived a day late.[1]

So how did this madness come about?

After losing by 267 runs in Perth, England made the obvious move of dropping their top wicket-taker. While Steven Finn had been dismissing batters regularly, he'd also been going for a few runs. The decision was therefore made to replace him with Tim Bresnan. The Yorkshireman's ability to bowl longer spells was considered especially useful as James Anderson was nursing a sore side that might mean a heavier workload for other bowlers.

As it was, Bresnan was only required to bowl 13 overs, which was 11 more than England's fourth bowler, Graeme Swann, because Australia were bowled out for 98 barely halfway through the day.

Reference has been made above to Australia not having batted dreadfully in the first three Tests. While this is not really untrue, if you were pushed to identify a moment when this particular implosion was foreshadowed, you could do worse than the start of the second Test, twenty-three days earlier.

It's rare to lose your captain for a golden duck from the fifth ball of a match and for that *not* to be the worst moment in the over – but that's what Australia had somehow achieved in Adelaide, where Ricky Ponting's herculean innings had been one ball longer than Simon Katich's.

At least Ponting got the opportunity to edge Anderson to slip. Fourth ball of the match, Shane Watson had called for a single that Katich didn't immediately agree

---

1   In contrast, Australians had by that point already experienced a compounding of their own Boxing Day morning hangovers, having witnessed events unfold before them.

with – a difference of opinion that resulted in the latter being run out by Trott without having faced a ball. Two overs later, it was 3/2 when Michael Clarke copied Ponting.

While on that occasion Mike Hussey and Brad Haddin had salvaged the innings,[2] in Melbourne on Boxing Day no salvage operation was forthcoming.

Chris Tremlett, a terrifying behemoth of a man who always looked like he was going to literally devour the batters, settled instead for dismissing them parsimoniously,[3] taking 4/26. For his part, Jimmy Anderson, his sore side apparently not debilitating, had Michaels Clarke and Hussey, Steve Smith and Mitchell Johnson all caught by wicketkeeper Matt Prior to secure figures of 4/44. (All ten Australian wickets fell to catches behind the wicket.)

The only batter to emerge in credit was Ryan Harris, who finished unbeaten on 10. An uptick in batting form was always likely, given he'd managed not just one but two golden ducks in Adelaide, and had followed that up with 3 and 1 in Perth. (This rapid rate of improvement meant a second-innings fifty was practically guaranteed.[4])

Okay, so that was the first innings of the match. But you know what they say: never judge a pitch until both teams have batted on it.

When Andrew Strauss and Alastair Cook walked off later that same day with the score on 0/157, it has to be said, it didn't feel like a 98 all out sort of a pitch. In fact, another 500-plus total seemed only marginally less likely than England's dead-cert retention of the Ashes.

A 500-plus total is duly what was delivered, built around Jonathan Trott's truly remorseless eight-hour 168 not out. Not too long after that, they'd again won a Test match by an innings.

Before the series began, England had notched only ten innings victories in Australia since their first such result in 1883. Just three of these had arrived since 1936, but they'd now added two more in the space of three weeks.

---

2 If not the match – an innings defeat can't really be presented as the outcome of a successful salvage operation.
3 A weirdly infrequently taken option among beasts who have this sort of air about them – cinematic dinosaurs and the like.
4 Or, as it turned out, an absent hurt.

Another week and another Test match and they'd added a third one after racking up 644 in Sydney.

At this point, the post-Perth assessment that normal England Ashes tour service was being resumed seemed just a little wide of the mark.

10

ELLYSE PERRY PERFORMS FEATS OF HYPERCOMPETENCE

AKA ELITE PERRY

Ellyse Perry, delighted but not surprised to have added levitation to the ever-lengthening list of skills she's mastered.

There is something fundamentally ridiculous about Ellyse Perry. Not in her demeanour, of course, which mostly exudes a very sensible air of 'Let's not muck about too much, ladies, we have a cricket match to dominate'.

Oh, sure, sometimes Perry has her humorous cricketing moments. That's not all that surprising. She's been playing international cricket since 2007. Over such a long period, you're bound to accidentally stumble into some nonsense every now and then.

For example, she famously celebrated reaching 198 at North Sydney Oval in 2017/18, having mistaken a lofted shot that fell just inside the boundary rope for one that fell the other side of it.

And, yes, there was also the time that she bounced out Lydia Greenway in the 2015 Ashes Test. England had been set 263 to win but had been playing for the draw after falling to 5/29. Greenway and Georgia Elwiss survived more than two hours before Greenway, having scored 16 off 137 balls, ducked under a Perry bouncer only for the delivery to somehow clip the top of leg stump.

Even those microscopic DNA fragments of silly cricket are, however, encased in the polytalented amber for which Perry has become famous. (As a benchmark of her absurd uber-handiness as a cricketer, Perry has a Test batting record that more or less aligns with Steve Smith's, and a bowling record that's roughly equivalent to that of Pat Cummins.[1])

The erroneous celebration was, to reiterate, for a Test double-century. The lowly bouncer dismissal was part of a match-winning 6/32.

The fundamental ridiculousness of Ellyse Perry, then, is her quite startling levels of cricketing hypercompetence. And perhaps the peak of Perry's ultra-proficiency in the sport came during the 2019 Ashes.

The first two ODIs of the multi-format series saw Perry functioning in standard all-rounder mode. In her opening spell of the first ODI, she dismissed both England openers, then trapped England captain Heather Knight LBW for a golden duck. England were 4/19 and the game was as good as done. (Although Australia made hard work of their chase of 178,

---

[1] She also scored a goal in the quarter-finals of the 2011 Football World Cup, Australia's most recent regular time World Cup finals goal until Sam Kerr's in 2023. A really rather useful athlete.

losing eight wickets in the process.) In the second ODI, Perry's contribution with the ball was a single lousy wicket in her first over (Amy Jones, for the second time in as many matches). But arriving at the crease at 2/17 in pursuit of 218, Perry top-scored with 62 from 79 deliveries as Australia cruised home.

So far, so above-averagely useful. But over the next two matches, Perry cranked up her omni-adeptness to quite extremely silly levels indeed.

In the third ODI, she didn't contribute much with the bat, making just 7. But Alyssa Healy and Meg Lanning helped Australia reach 7/269. The target of 270 would have been a record chase for England, had they been successful.

England were not, however, successful – which was due almost entirely to Perry. In her first over, a wicket maiden, she dismissed Jones yet again. (Across the series to that point, Jones had faced eight balls from Perry, hit one boundary and been dismissed three times.)

In Perry's second over, she had Tammy Beaumont trapped LBW, then Sarah Taylor caught behind first ball. Her third and fourth overs went shamefully wicketless, but she bookended her fifth over with the wickets of Heather Knight, caught behind, and Danni Wyatt, trapped in front. So Perry had 5/12 from her opening five-over spell, which became 7/22 from her full ten overs. England were bowled out for 75.

The figures were the best ever by an Australian woman in ODIs, earning her an obvious Player of the Match award. Her effort also led to the press asking Perry after the match if she considered herself to be the best all-rounder in the game.

'You can call me what you like,' she replied. 'But I'm not sure that's the case. I honestly think today just went my way, which is nice.'

You know what also just went her way (which is nice)? The next match, where the magnitude of the falseness of Perry's modesty was brutally exposed. For, not content with a record ODI performance with the ball, she now chipped in with a record Test performance with the bat.

She scored 116 in Australia's first innings of 8/420 (declared). That knock (on the back of her prematurely celebrated 213 not out in the previous series) meant that she went a total of 655 balls between Test dismissals, scoring 329 runs, both numbers a record in women's Tests. Presumably annoyed at her carelessness on that

655th ball, caught by Knight off Laura Marsh, Perry started again, scoring 76 not out from 144 balls in the second innings. This was the start of another streak, in which she added 163 runs across four innings and 384 balls before her next Test match dismissal, in 2022. In other words, there was a stretch of more than a thousand Test match deliveries, in which Perry was dismissed once and scored almost 500 runs.

This is not normal behaviour from a cricketer.

As if to keep in practice for this long-haul Test record, she batted thrice in the T20 leg of the 2019 Ashes, and was not out on all three occasions, with scores of 7 not out, 47 not out and 60 not out. She also got another four balls in at poor old Amy Jones across the T20s, dismissing her one last time. Cruel stuff. Cruel, funny stuff.

> **ACTIVITY CORNER**
>
> 1. Determine what aspect of cricket you are most skilled at (running between the wickets, putting your pads on quickly, twirling your bat in a dismissive fashion, et cetera).
> 2. Spend years honing that skill to the peak of your abilities.
> 3. To three decimal places, calculate how annoying it is that Ellyse Perry will always be better at that skill than you.

9
JIMMY AND MONTY SAVE ENGLAND

AKA TICKING OFF MINUTES AND PONTING

Aleem Dar reminds James Anderson and Monty Panesar what the big hand and little hand respectively indicate.

What is batting all about? It's all about scoring runs, isn't it?

Except when it's not.

If there is one batter England fans would choose to have at the crease to bat out a draw, it is surely Paul Collingwood. He always seemed like a batter imbued with that particular type of self-contained confidence that manifests in deeds, not peacocking.

In 2008, he earned himself the nickname 'Brigadier Block' after scoring two runs off 50 balls on the final day of a Test against New Zealand in Hamilton. That match ended in a defeat, but in 2009/10 he played two quite gloriously lumpen innings in South Africa that helped secure nine-wickets-down draws. A 99-ball 26 in Centurion was one thing, but the leaving/missing case study at Newlands – when he made only 40 runs in more than four and a half hours of batting, and looked like getting out to Dale Steyn every other ball – was something else again.

Remember too that even in the 'Amazing Adelaide' Test of 2006 (have we not mentioned that yet?), Collingwood was the one man unbeaten when Shane Warne wove his cataclysmic spell.

With his one-inch backlift and utter refusal to play attacking shots, Brigadier Block had a game plan for batting for a draw on a tough final-day pitch.

Explaining his methodology to *The Independent*, he said: 'The attitude is that if anything is wide, leave it; anything short, drop your hands; and anything on the stumps, block it. You keep it as simple as possible. I'm out there to waste as many balls as possible.'

In 2009, Collingwood batted for six hours and wasted 245 balls to make 74 runs in the first Ashes Test at Swalec Stadium, as England desperately tried to cling on for a draw.

He arrived at the crease at 3/31 in the second innings, with his team still 208 runs behind Australia's brutally protracted first innings 6/674.[1] It was the first morning of the final day. There was a lot of time to kill.

By drinks, England were 4/55 and by lunch 5/102. At tea, it was 7/169 and the second new ball was just nine overs away. When that accounted for the home side's last competent batter,

---

1 No fewer than four batters had made hundreds: Simon Katich, Ricky Ponting, Marcus North and Brad Haddin.

Graeme Swann, Collingwood was joined by the first incompetent one, James Anderson, and together they saw out another 13 overs before disaster struck. ('Disaster', in this instance, being Peter Siddle.)

What is Paul Collingwood's greatest weakness? Well, England were six runs behind at this point and the distracting concept of run-scoring had therefore reared its ugly head. Every run they got ahead would be a run that Australia would then have to score to win the game – not to mention the fact that two overs would be lost for the change of innings.

Collingwood therefore took it upon himself to – horror of horrors! – play a shot. Pushing off the back foot, he sliced the ball to gully, where Mike Hussey first palmed it into the air and then gathered it at the second attempt.

To give some sense of how utterly catastrophic this moment was for England fans, it's worth highlighting Collingwood's own reaction when he revisited the match for a Sky Sports lockdown 'watchalong' in 2020.

'I've gone!' he exclaimed, hands reflexively clasping his head the way so many of us do when a crucial wicket falls.

People don't generally react to replays in the same way they react to live sport. Pained exclamations more usually emerge from our mouths when the occurrence is a surprise. Given that Collingwood was watching footage of his own actions, you'd think he might have had an inkling what was on the way – but really this is the measure of the moment. It was a reaction impossible to suppress. Collingwood had gone and all hope with him, because he was about to be replaced at the crease by Monty Panesar.

If there is one batter England fans would not want at the crease to bat out a draw, it is Monty Panesar.

Panesar was an excellent cricketer – an overall assessment that is not merely shaped by his bowling but wholly based on it. As a fielder, he was lamentable.[2] As a batter, he was execrable.

Oddly, he quite often looked good. That is to say, his technique looked

---

2   If there has ever been a more tense moment in Test cricket than Panesar standing under an MS Dhoni skyer during England's 2006 tour of India, then you wouldn't want to experience it. This is largely because it occurred just two balls after he had (somehow) missed a previous MS Dhoni skyer by three metres. If there has ever been a more unlikely catch taken than when Panesar refused to let all that pressure exacerbate his extraordinary fielding incompetence, we can't begin to imagine the circumstances.

pretty tidy and his cover drive in particular would sometimes manifest as a real textbook affair. Looking good wasn't Panesar's problem. Hitting the ball was the issue.

In this sense, he was almost an anti-Collingwood. Panesar's speciality was a beautifully straight and controlled forward defensive where the bat came down either 20 to 30 centimetres away from where the ball was or a full second after it had passed (or sometimes both).

He was, in short, not the man you wanted arriving at the crease with 69 deliveries to see off and just the one wicket in hand.[3]

Not that anyone knew there were 69 deliveries remaining. Test cricket isn't so accommodating as to let you know what your exact objective is. With an Ashes Test at stake, the goal was to bat for, oh, probably eleven or twelve overs? Maybe more? I dunno – ask me again in a bit and I'll see how much time's left.

According to Anderson, 'It felt a little bit mad at times, out in the middle, trying to get information from the umpire. How long are we actually going to be out here for? Is it overs? Is it time? And no one seemed to know the answer.'

All anyone was really sure of was that if either Jimmy or Monty got out, Australia won. So they had to not get out for somewhere around thirty-five minutes.

This didn't seem especially likely when Monty first walked out, equipped with what Anderson described as 'the widest eyes you had ever seen'. Quite apart from the two men's limited batting ability, there was also the small matter of their running between the wickets to contend with. 'The calling wasn't overly great,' remembered Anderson.

When Panesar got off the mark with a single, the crowd as good as gave him a standing ovation. Not long after, Anderson fluked a boundary that gave England the lead. From then on, almost anything that happened – whether runs or dot balls – felt priceless to England.

Given the ticking clock, even events that interrupted play had their value. Twice in the space of five minutes, 12th man Bilal Shafayat went on to give Panesar and Anderson towels and spare gloves – the second time accompanied

---

[3] Although obviously anyone who pushed Jimmy Anderson up to the number ten spot was at least familiar with a scenario where his team had only one wicket in hand.

by physio Steve McCaig[4] so that the batters could have another time-wasting option.

Anderson said he believed they were meant to be his spare gloves, only 'I didn't often carry two pairs'.

Australia captain Ricky Ponting spoke angrily about these incursions after the game, saying, 'They had changed gloves before, so I'm not sure they were going to be too sweaty after one over.'

England captain Andrew Strauss's response was conspicuously worded: 'If Ricky's angry, that's a shame,' he said. 'I don't think we were deliberately trying to waste a huge amount of time.'

Not a *huge* amount of time …

Either way, by hook or by crook (in fact, there were zero hooks and, despite Ponting's protests, only the most minor of time-wasting crookedness), Anderson and Panesar eventually reached their target – the close of play. The climactic moment entirely passed pretty much everyone by, with quite a lot of confused milling about at the end of one particular over before the umpires eventually confirmed it was the end of the match.

Is batting all about scoring runs? If you had never seen cricket before and switched on your TV that evening, you would have been greeted by the sights and sounds of a Cardiff crowd spending half an hour or so cheering increasingly more wildly each time the two worst batters in the England team deliberately left the ball.

---

[4] McCaig was an Aussie who had grown up idolising Ricky Ponting. What a treat it must have been to enter the field of play and get, in Anderson's words, 'an absolute volley' from his hero.

8

JONNY BAIRSTOW LEAVES HIS GROUND

AKA CAREY, CAREY, QUITE CONTRARY

Alex Carey and Pat Cummins learn that the latter will fulfil his childhood dream of penning a foreword for an irreverent Ashes book and immediately celebrate the good news.

One of the most memorably absurd moments of the 2023 Ashes came during the Lord's Test.

You probably remember it (this, after all, is what 'memorable' means): that time when Jonny Bairstow unexpectedly wandered off when he arguably shouldn't have, setting in motion a series of events that went viral across the cricketing world.

Obviously, the moment to which we're referring is when a couple of 'Just Stop Oil' protesters invaded the ground prior to the second over of the Test, hurling orange powder near Stuart Broad's run-up, before the England wicketkeeper took matters into his own gloved hands. Bairstow lifted up the nearest trespasser, placed him under his arm like a large, environmentally disgruntled umbrella and carried him off the ground. The sight of Bairstow providing a no-nonsense volunteer security service turned out to be, in fact, extremely nonsensical. A very silly moment on all kinds of levels. No wonder the protester wrapped beneath Bairstow's arms raised his fist to the sky in triumph.

Ah, but perhaps that's not the memorably absurd moment you were recalling. Maybe you were instead casting your mind back to the moment in the Test when the startling behaviour of one of the Australians elicited a ... shall we say, impassioned response from the Lord's members.

Remember? When Nathan Lyon, having torn his calf performing a seemingly harmless piece of outfielding, nevertheless hobbled out to bat at number eleven in the second innings, much to the admiration and respectful applause of the members in the Long Room.

Lyon was playing in his hundredth consecutive Test, a testament not just to his fitness but also to his value within the Australian set-up. Usually, that value was measured by his contributions with the ball, but here, as in the first Test, Lyon chipped in with the bat. Hopping around comically on one leg in defiance of his captain and coach (to be clear, they had been against him batting at all, rather than specifically the hopping variant in which he was indulging), he added 18 runs with Mitchell Starc for the last wicket. It was a not-inconsiderable tally, given that Australia ultimately won the match by just 43 runs.

Maybe, however, that's not the memorably absurd moment you were thinking of either. In which case, let's cut the nonsense and dig into the controversy that erupted when the umpires made a ruling on a dismissal that, while technically correct, was so outside the ordinary that it had the team that fell afoul of the decision fuming at the wrongly perceived injustice of it all.

You know – the Starc 'catch'. With Lyon having helped set England 371 runs, the pace portion of the Australian attack was now asked to seal the win without his spinning assistance. No problem whatsoever. Starc and Pat Cummins swiftly had England 4/45, before a fightback from Bens Stokes and Duckett saw England through to stumps. Although only barely. A skied chance from the latter in the last minutes of play was safely caught by Starc at fine leg, only for it to be unsafely uncaught when he dragged the ball on the ground as he slid to a halt.

The left-arm quick was furious with Duckett's reprieve. 'You can't walk off now if you get caught,' Starc advised his teammates as he entered the dressing room at the end of play. 'Just hang around and wait for the replay.'

But the decision was correct. Starc might have been in full control of the ball and his movement, but the replay showed he had clearly neglected to turn his hand around to keep the ball away from the grass. It was the kind of carelessness that might have been overlooked by less diligent officials, but third umpire Marais Erasmus was not going to let Starc's slide slide.

But hey, what if that's not your most memorably absurd moment from this Test either?

Okay, fine. Let's get to it: the final-day moment that merges all three of those ridiculous 2023 Lord's Test prototypes into a sublime Frankensteinian piece of cricketing nonsense. Bairstow wandering off. An unexpected act from an Australian. Unjustified fury over a perfectly correct decision from the umpires. Let's talk about Alex Carey's stumping of Jonny Bairstow.

It's almost impossible to find anything new to say about this ridiculous moment, given the relentless coverage of the wicket and its aftermath at the time. (Which, of course, is why we've spent most of this piece procrastinating with other gloriously absurd moments from that Test.)

The bare facts are these. Bairstow had made a habit of regularly leaving his crease after he'd left a delivery but before the ball was dead. Cummins had noticed this and relayed the observation to Carey. The next time Bairstow ducked under a Cameron Green bouncer, Carey immediately underarmed the ball at the stumps.

With the ball in flight, Bairstow walked out of his crease. The ball hit the stumps. The Australians appealed. The umpires sent the decision upstairs. Erasmus confirmed Bairstow was out.

The aftermath was less clear-cut, but again the details are well trodden. Bairstow looked utterly baffled by the fate that had befallen him. The crowd began to boo. Broad (who else?) arrived at the crease to fan the flames.[1] Stokes's flames were so sufficiently fanned that he launched a Headingley-esque counterattack that almost snatched the Test for England. The Lord's members hurled abuse at the Australians when they entered the Long Room for lunch (eliciting Marcus Harris's perhaps definitive summary of the entire incident: 'I was like, "You wrote the rules, you fucking idiots."'). Lunch itself devolved into the Australians stifling giggles as David Warner mocked England's attempts to claim the high ground. Piers Morgan made a predictable pillock of himself by blathering on about the Spirit of Cricket. Brendon McCullum made the grim ruling that he would no longer have a drink with the Australians. Carey was falsely accused of an illicit haircut. The notion of a 'moral Ashes' was birthed and used as a comic crutch long after it ceased being interesting or novel.

And on and on and on it went until the heat death of the universe.

The moment cemented Bairstow's legacy in the minds of most Australian fans as a slapstick comedy figure.

England fans, understandably, have a more nuanced and sympathetic view of Bairstow. And Bairstow's biggest fan was perhaps Stokes himself, who just a summer earlier had seen his keeper hit the purplest patch of his career, hitting century after century in improbable run chases to validate the skipper's brand-new Bazball approach.

It came as no surprise, then, two Tests later, with England well on top in Manchester[2] thanks to a blistering 189 from Crawley, that Stokes allowed

---

1 Broad, the magnificently ridiculous showman, emphatically shouted 'in' every time he grounded his bat. He would later observe of himself that he 'seemed to carry on like that for hours', adding, 'It was so petulant, but it was my frustration and it ignited the series.' Yes, Stuart. Yes, it did.
2 One of the more amusing aspects of the 2023 Ashes is that four of the Tests were won and lost by incredibly tight margins, but the sole Test where one side clearly dominated was the one that ended in a draw. Cricket, eh?

Bairstow to bat on for a redemptive century.

With rain forecast for the fourth and fifth days, there was a case for England to resume bowling as soon as possible to take the necessary wickets to win the Test. Especially since Australia had examined the forecast and, needing only a draw to retain the Ashes, lengthened their batting (quite literally, replacing Todd Murphy with the notoriously tall Green as a second all-rounder alongside Mitchell Marsh).

Stokes was having none of this declaration talk, however.[3] There were multiple ways to skin a cat, and if one form of feline-flaying gave Bairstow a chance for a ton, that was the one he was taking. (As it turned out, it would have made no difference whether England declared or not. With incessant final-day rain transforming Old Trafford into the not out Australian all-rounders,[4] time simply ran out for England.)

But Bairstow's century? That proved just out of reach too, although he ran out of partners rather than time, stranded on 99 not out when England were bowled out for 592.

Jonny Bairstow, once again, had found himself one small step away from where he wanted/needed to be.

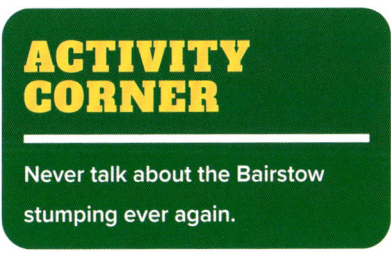

ACTIVITY CORNER

Never talk about the Bairstow stumping ever again.

---

3 Once bitten by Cummins's match-winning bat, twice shy, presumably (see No. 48).
4 A green marsh.

7

AMAZING ADELAIDE, THE TEST THAT NEVER HAPPENED

AKA ENGLAND'S WORST EVER NUMBER FOUR

Paul Collingwood foolishly paves the way for an Australia victory by scoring a mere 206.

It's not often, as a batter, that you come in for huge criticism after scoring a double-hundred in one innings and remaining unbeaten in the second, but cricket's a funny old game.[1]

Paul Collingwood was rarely the first name on the England team sheet, and not solely because the selectors preferred to warm up their biros with shorter ones, like Bell, Cook or Root. As often as not, for most of his career, he was picked with a certain ambivalence – a temporary inclusion until someone better came along.

This insipid shoulder-shrugging acceptance extended to the media as well, where what compliments he did attract were generally served backhand. 'He makes the most of his talent' was the most common – the implication being that he only had so much to make use of in the first place.

Collingwood's was therefore a Test career of almost perpetual jeopardy, and going into the 2006 Ashes, his position was fairly typical. With just two Test centuries under his belt and a reputation at the time as more of a bits-and-pieces one-day cricketer, his confidence wasn't exactly being buoyed by conspicuous selectorial conviction.

But despite this widespread view of him as a rather fortunate utility cricketer who'd benefited from an uncomplaining willingness to carry the drinks on previous Test tours, Michael Vaughan's injury and Marcus Trescothick's departure from the tour due to a 'recurrence of a stress-related illness' meant he was now set to move up the batting order to the pivotal number four spot. 'Well, who else?' seemed to be the vibe about this promotion (and indeed his inclusion in the first place).

The Australian press responded to the change in role much as you'd imagine, by asking whether he was England's worst ever number four batter. Again, the subtext wasn't hard to read: yeah, he probably is.

Collingwood had actually made 96 in the final innings of the first Test, but nobody was much impressed. England had been chasing the small matter of 648 to win, so his dismissal for 5 earlier in the match was taken as far more representative of his value to the team. Getting stumped off Shane Warne when he was within one shot of a hundred in the second innings didn't help his reputation much either.

---

1   A ridiculous one, even.

'He just tossed it up and lured us down and I missed it,' reflected Collingwood matter-of-factly afterwards.

So it was that he entered the second Test, at Adelaide, still with just two hundreds to his name and still widely regarded as England's worst ever number four.[2]

Andrew Flintoff won the toss and batted, and Collingwood again made the most of his talent, finishing the day agonisingly poised on 98 not out. Early the next morning, he shrugged off poor sleep – 'I felt like I was up every 20 minutes' – to successfully add that coveted extra digit.[3] He must have really enjoyed raising his bat too, because he then immediately scored another hundred.

It's easy to forget in light of what followed (read on, friends!), but this was, in its way, one of the most forceful rebuttals in Ashes history. England's worst ever number four? Try England's first double-centurion in Australia for seventy years.

As displays of grit go, it was hard to match. Collingwood waged war on the Australia attack (perhaps 'waged Waugh' would be more appropriate, given his tenacity was reminiscent of the former Australia captain's), to the extent that Shane Warne conceded 1/167 – his most expensive Test innings – while Glenn McGrath's 0/107 was the only time in his career that he conceded over 100 without taking a wicket.

Collingwood's innings was built on a 310-run stand with Kevin Pietersen, who made 158. (One of three career 158s, weirdly – and his second against Australia in little more than a year.)

Flintoff declared on 6/551, only for Australia to respond with 513 all out after hundreds by Ricky Ponting and Michael Clarke. (Does anyone in the world remember that Matthew Hoggard took seven wickets in that innings? If they do, that person almost certainly goes by the name of Matthew Hoggard.)

Day four ended not that weirdly, with England on 1/59 after 19 overs. Day five, then, unfolded fully weirdly, because by lunch England were 5/89.

---

2   We don't know about 'worst', but England's least successful number four was probably Mark Butcher, who batted there twice but failed to score a run. A word too for Dean Headley, who made four runs in four innings of nightwatchery, with a highest (and lowest) score of 1.
3   To his score – he didn't grow an extra finger.

It's worth taking a minute to dissect those numbers. At the start of that final day, England were as near as, dammit, 100 ahead with nine wickets in hand. They then scored 30 runs in 28 overs while losing five wickets.

One thing was for sure: England weren't going to die wondering. They were in fact going to die paralysed and consumed from within by parasitic wasp larvae – a protracted and agonising death about which they could apparently do nothing.

After lunch, it was more of the same: another 30 runs scored – this time in 26 overs, which also brought the final four wickets.

Adelaide 2006 is sometimes remembered as a collapse, but that rather understates the duration of the fall. Yes, England were all out for 129 on a pitch where runs had been plentiful, but they were all out for 129 in 73 overs.

England's shotlessness was such that Glenn McGrath decided he'd just bowl cutters, with Adam Gilchrist keeping up to the stumps. Warne might have been the one to induce the paralysis, but it wasn't a quick kill. His 4/49 required him to bowl 32 overs.

The key wicket was Pietersen's, an arcing leg-break that kicked back so sharply it passed behind the batter's legs and hit his off stump. Collingwood was on 0 off seven balls at the time and responded by almost entirely renouncing run-scoring.

When Flintoff was dismissed, he had reached 1 off 19 balls. When Geraint Jones was out, he had scored 5 off 54. A late four took him to 22 off 119 balls, and that was where he was stranded when James Anderson became the final wicket to fall. Unbowed, unbeaten, undefeated, or the guiltiest contributor to the only scenario in which Australia still had enough time to reach their victory target?

When Australia knocked off the 168 runs required inside 33 overs, a lot of people felt it was the latter.

Unforgettable stuff – except in England, where fans have long made a conscious effort to convince the world that this Test match never in fact took place.[4]

Memory, hey? The game in which Shane Warne returned the most

---

4   To this day, many England supporters will simply shrug and ask, in straight-faced faux-confusion, why there was no Ashes Test played in Adelaide that summer.

expensive bowling figures of his Test career is now remembered as one of his greatest triumphs, while Paul Collingwood's highest Test score in the same game will forever be obscured by the blame he attracted for England's eventual defeat.

Worst ever number four was a bit unfair, though. And at least he was committed to the job. Damien Martyn watched all this unfold from his vantage point in Australia's middle order and then immediately stopped playing cricket forever.

6

SHANE WATSON IS DISMISSED

AKA WATTO WAY TO GO

An oblivious Shane Watson celebrates his century, unaware that he will soon be dismissed in ridiculous fashion.

Ho ho ho! you're probably thinking, if you've read the heading to this piece before starting on the content (as more than 70 per cent of readers do). *What kind of ridiculous mess has Watto's massive front pad got him into this time?*

You may well also be rubbing your hands together in gleeful anticipation of how Shane Watson's infamous forearm-punching reviewing-fist might likewise contribute to the moment, desperately calling on DRS, only to be comically denied by the third umpire.

It's entirely understandable you might make this assumption. Nobody in the history of Test cricket was dismissed LBW more reliably than Watson, who succumbed to the mode of dismissal on 27.3 per cent of the occasions he lost his wicket.

In Ashes cricket, he was even more prone to plonking down his big front foot right in front of the stumps and allowing the ball to cannon into it. He was out thirty-five times against England, and fourteen of those dismissals (a solid 40 per cent) were LBW.

Watson began his Ashes career in 2009, returning to the Test team after a six-month absence for the third Test at Edgbaston. He made 62 at the top of the order, before being out LBW to Graham Onions on the first ball of the second day. (Marvellously, he was also out at 10.59am, which meant he was technically out before the scheduled start of play. Onions then had Mike Hussey bowled without playing a shot from the second ball of the day – a commendably silly start to a day of cricket.)

Watson ended his Ashes career (and, indeed, his Test career), six years later, in the first Test of the 2015 series at Cardiff. He was LBW in both innings. Reviewed in both innings. Had his review denied in both innings. A fitting farewell(bw) to the King of the Front Pad.

And yet, in cruel defiance of the odds, the dismissal we're about to discuss here is not a Shane Watson LBW. Instead, we're off to the WACA in the summer of 2013/14 for one of the silliest morning sessions in Ashes history.

England were on the brink of surrendering the Ashes they'd easily retained just six months earlier. Having been completely Mitchell Johnsoned in the first two Tests, Alastair Cook's men had now carelessly allowed Australia's weird leg-spinner, Steve

Smith, to score a century against them in the first innings of this third Test.[1]

A lacklustre batting effort in reply saw England concede a 134-run lead on the first innings. By the end of the third day, Australia had extended that advantage to 369 with seven wickets still in hand, and Watson and Smith both at the crease.

The fourth day, therefore, saw Australia batting for a declaration. Watson was at his brutal best that morning. Resuming on 29, he hit 14 from the first over of the day, eventually adding 74 runs from just 42 balls. It's easy (and fun!) to remember Watson's comical dismissals. But in between the wickets, the man could give it an absolute bloody thump.

In this knock of 103, he absolute-bloody-thumped eleven fours and five sixes, including one where he was caught on the boundary by a leaping Tim Bresnan, only for the Yorkshireman to land beyond the rope, moving Watson to 96. Three (legal[2]) deliveries later, he had his century. Two balls after that, he was out. And out in a manner that, with all due respect to his incredible LBW feats, was the most ridiculous dismissal of his career.

England were 465 runs behind and doomed. The Ashes were surely gone. Nevertheless, Bresnan returned to the bowling crease, the over after having 'caught' Watson for six and immediately caught the top edge of his bat as the almighty all-rounder attempted another contemptuous pull shot.

The ball went straight up. Ian Bell, fielding at cover, settled under it. Watson dropped his head and half-heartedly trotted down the pitch, far enough to at least keep George Bailey on strike, back when the Laws of Cricket permitted such a thing. (To be clear, the laws didn't mention Bailey specifically. Anybody could be kept on strike in this fashion.)

Bell, meanwhile, also dropped his head – but not before dropping the ball. Disgusted with himself, the fielder turned his back on the dropped ball and immediately sulked off. Bresnan, correctly furious, picked it up and threw down the stumps at the non-striker's end.

---

1   Boosting his average to just over 35. Good work, kid! You keep at it.
2   He also got to witness the always ridiculous sight of a delivery that resulted in five wides.

Bresnan might not even have been trying to run Watson out. He might well have just been expelling his pent-up rage with an angry throw. He did, however, run Watson out, because Watson was still in the middle of the pitch, feeling sad about being caught, when he wasn't caught. This abject disappointment at almost certainly being dismissed ensured that even when he wasn't dismissed, he would be. That, dear reader, is the gift of Shane Watson.

Bell, his back still turned to the play, didn't realise a wicket had taken place. He strode off in one direction. Watson, miles out of his ground when the furious Bresnan threw down the stumps, was running off to the pavilion the other way. Bresnan stood between them, still livid at not taking a wicket even as he was taking a wicket.

It was one of the most ridiculous dismissals in Ashes history, and it set a suitably nonsense tone for the rest of the morning session. A few overs later, Bailey hit 28 runs off a Jimmy Anderson over to give the bowler the record for the (equal) most expensive over in Test history. (Stuart Broad surpassed him in 2022, inexplicably going for 35 runs while bowling to, um, Jasprit Bumrah.)

Michael Clarke declared after that record over, and then the very next thing to happen in the Test was, as per tradition, the first ball of the England innings. This, too, was world-class absurdity.

England needed to bat for two days to keep the Ashes alive (or score 504 to win). Captain Alastair Cook was at the crease, willing and ready to lead from the front in his 100th Test. So, obviously, Ryan Harris ran in and bowled a ball that has since been decreed by the Cricinfo website to be the Ball of the 21st Century. (So far, at least. We assume the good folk at Cricinfo don't have access to time travel.)

The ball, delivered right arm over the wicket, swung in the air towards the stumps, pitching perilously close to a classic WACA crack without quite hitting it. Despite missing the crack, the ball still seamed away from Cook's perfectly sensible back-foot defence and then started to *swing* away in addition to the movement off the seam – just enough to clip the top of off stump.

It was a preposterous and worthy successor to Shane Warne's Ball of the 20th Century. Harris celebrated by running around in random directions like a toddler who'd had one too many juices. Although perhaps it was not random. Perhaps his constant swerving and changing of direction as he ran around in celebration was, in fact, an attempt to re-enact the trajectory of the ball.

Regardless, a fitting climax to a morning of utter cricket nonsense.

5

STOKES THE HEADINGLEY HERO

AKA STOKES THE LEEDS LIABILITY

Headingley 2019 is rightly remembered for the brilliance of Ben Stokes. What's often forgotten is that, for rather a lot of that match, he was something of a liability for England.

Joe Root won the toss and asked Australia to bat in damp, difficult conditions. They were bowled out for 179. Jofra Archer took 6/45 off 17.1 overs. Stokes took 1/45 off 9.

The one wicket he took was that of top scorer Marnus Labuschagne, who failed to lay bat on one that slammed into the top of his pad and would have gone on to hit middle halfway up. It is, however, possible that Labuschagne only missed the ball because he was more accustomed to playing at deliveries that at some point made contact with the pitch.

In reply, England were all out for 67. And no one was more culpable than Stokes, who just about managed to edge a barely reachable wide half-volley from James Pattinson. Despite the grave implications of the dismissal – it took England from 3/34 to 4/34 – the shot was sufficiently ludicrous that commentator Ebony Rainford-Brent couldn't quite get through the words 'a wide, rank delivery' during the replay without struggling to suppress a laugh.

A lot of players' pride would have been pricked by what Stokes had delivered thus far in the match, and many would dutifully resolve to make amends. Given the way the game was panning out, however, almost all would pencil in that penance for the next Test match. Perhaps the most ridiculous aspect of Ben Stokes's Headingley performance was that, having given Australia a colossal head start, he for some reason set about trying to win the same Test match, continuing to strive for victory even when it honestly made zero sense.

When Stokes came on to bowl in the second innings, Australia were 197 runs ahead with seven wickets in hand. He'd basically bowled a load of dross in the first innings but now reverted to being a Test bowler seemingly through willpower alone.

In his fourth over, he expressed his distaste for both head starts and Head starts by yorking Travis. He wasn't easy to score off either, and by the end of an eight-over spell had achieved very respectable figures of 1/12. His replacement at the Football Stand End was Archer, but when the fast bowler succumbed to cramp after just four balls, it was Stokes who completed the over. The four-ball breather must have had a really significant effect, because he then continued from that same end for another 16 overs.

The spell did, admittedly, span an overnight, but that's statistically quite likely when you bowl 24.2 overs pretty much in a row. He finished with 3/56, having somehow found the strength to bounce out Matthew Wade and Pat Cummins.

Australia finished 246 all out, which meant England needed 359 to win. The only team to have made so many to win a Test on English shores had Don Bradman in it. That one had been at Headingley too.[1] Bradman's Australia hadn't been bowled out for 67 in the first innings either.

England had never once made so many to win a Test, and at 2/15 that didn't seem at all likely to change. However, Joes Root and Denly plodded the home team up to 3/141 off 59.3 overs, at which point Stokes replaced Denly at the crease.

Then things *really* changed.

Because, against all the odds, England slowed down even further. At stumps, they were 3/156 off 72 overs and Stokes had scored 2 off 50 balls, with half his rally arriving by accident from an inside edge. By the time Root was out for 77 the next morning, Stokes had gaily skipped his way to 3 off 67 balls. Perhaps regretting the wild single that had so fatefully put Root back on strike, he then played out six more dot balls before finally hitting his first boundary off the 74th delivery he faced.

Whether you're English or Australian, you'll have some notion of how this Stokes innings went, but it most likely won't be this bit you're thinking of. It was a crucial period, though. This was no whackaday T20 innings where the batter swings from the off. The extreme madness of its climax can only be fully appreciated when set against the equal-but-opposite madness of how it began.

Everyone remembers the part when he mimicked Ian Botham. It's not quite so widely remembered that, by then, he'd already done a fantastic impersonation of Chris Tavaré.

The shift from one to the other is what was most incredible. Stokes might argue he was building the foundations for a towering innings, but most tall edifices have lower floors – construction doesn't generally move directly from the groundworks to the rooftop terrace. Batters frequently talk

---

[1] A lot of weird shit happens at Headingley – and some of it on the field of play.

about going through the gears, but this was Michael Knight reaching for KITT's turbo boost while pulling out of his driveway.[2]

The partnership with Jonny Bairstow was what passed for the transitional period – a flickering thing where both modes of batting tried to coexist, dot balls occasionally making way for fours and even an unexpected six.

When Bairstow was out, England's last recognised batter, Jos Buttler, came in. With 103 needed for victory, Buttler's partner ran him out. Stokes the Liability was apparently still present in Leeds. The next partnership, with Chris Woakes, was worth eight runs, and while Stokes then put on 25 with Archer, even that mediocre effort was swiftly undermined when Stuart Broad was out second ball for a duck.

That meant England needed 73 runs when number eleven Jack Leach walked out.

'Jack has got some serious bollocks,' remarked Stokes afterwards. These earnest testes helped the spinner block and leave the ball like a champion. They also gave him the strength to repeatedly ask the bowler – and everyone else – to wait a moment while he de-steamed his glasses.

Whenever Leach was on strike, Stokes stood stock-still at the opposite end, with no intention of running. Sometimes he squatted. At times he stared at the ground, unable to watch. Then, when it was his turn to face, he hit sixes.

The first scoring shot of the partnership went straight over both bowler Nathan Lyon's head and the boundary rope. Long-off came a bit straighter in response, but Stokes hit the same shot again in the spinner's next over, with the same result. Four balls later, he fell over while playing a reverse slog sweep, but that too went for six.

A hustled single, a bit of cramp, some polished lenses and it was time for another one to go the distance, this time from an on-the-move ramp shot off Pat Cummins.

Cricket being cricket, the crowd's roars for Leach's forward defensives were almost as loud, but there were

---

[2] If you're too young to know *Knight Rider*, all you need to know is that the talking car had a pair of rocket boosters mounted just behind the front tyres. (Yeah, I know! Man, what a show.)

'Arms out if you've just miraculously stolen a Test for England.'

eight moments that day that stood out as warranting a bit of extra volume.³

1. Stokes's hundred, which barely registered with the man himself. A vague hand wave at the dressing room was the only real acknowledgement, and even that came across as less of a 'thanks' and more of a 'sit down, let me get on with this'.

2. A six into the Western Terrace off the third ball of a Josh Hazlewood over after he'd hit the first and second deliveries for four and six, respectively. At this point the delirium was so great that commentator Mark Nicholas said, 'No way, man!' There was surely no one on this earth less likely to voice the words 'No way, man!' than Mark Nicholas, which is a measure of just how crazy things had got.

3. Marcus Harris dropping him at third man on 116. (There were several misfields after this as the pressure built. Crowds love a misfield in these situations.)

4. With eight runs needed to win, Stokes went for another six over long-off fielder Labuschagne. It barely – *barely* – cleared him. This was a Schrödinger's lofted drive. In the short moments the ball was in the air, this colossal Test match felt simultaneously won and lost for both teams, with all possible resultant emotions mushrooming within everyone all at once.

5. Two balls after that, one shot from victory, Leach all but completed the single that would have secured at least a tie ... only to realise that Stokes wasn't actually running. With the non-striker half a pitch from safety, the throw went to the bowler's end. Terminal, you'd think, but as Lyon's hands darted towards the stumps, he realised they did not have the ball in them.

6. The very next ball, Stokes swept and missed and was rapped on the pad. Umpire Joel Wilson said not out, which was bad news for Australia because it should have been out and they'd burnt their last review

---

3   A peek behind the curtain here: this actually started out as just two moments, but as we revisited events, we found the partnership had other ideas.

the previous over on one that very obviously wasn't.

7. Three balls into the next over, bowled by Cummins, Jack Leach decided it was high time to score his first and only run, and in so doing levelled the scores.

8. A ball later, the victory: a moment of almost unmatchable catharsis as that tsunami of tension – days in the making – finally broke with a Stokes back-foot bludgeon for four.

England, all out for 67 in their first innings and chasing 359, had won. Ben Stokes, who had thrown his wicket away in the first innings and bowled a preposterous 24-over spell in Australia's second, had done it.

He was on 61 when Leach came in. He was on 135 at the finish. He scored those 74 runs in 45 balls, after beginning the very same innings with three runs in 73 balls.

Leach was on 0 when he came in. He was on 1 at the finish. He too was a vital hero for England – because the Ashes is, above all, ridiculous.

4

IAN BOTHAM PERFORMS LUDICROUS FEATS OF HEROISM

AKA ALEC BEDSER'S INSPIRED MAN MANAGEMENT

Ian Botham demonstrates black-and-white photography's ability to diminish the visibility of armpit stains.

There was one big question ahead of the 1981 Headingley Test: could Ian Botham recover a bit of form now he was no longer captain?

There was an even bigger question afterwards: WTF was that?

The bare facts of this match are well-worn, so let's scoot through them quickly. Australia made 9/401. England responded with 174 all out and then collapsed to 7/135 following on. At this point Botham hit 149 not out off 148 balls, adding 221 for the final three wickets. This meant Australia needed 130 for victory, but Bob Willis momentarily forgot how to bowl no balls and took 8/43 to secure a beyond-unlikely victory for England. Rod Marsh and Dennis Lillee went down to the bookmaker's to collect their winnings. No one banned them for life.

The whole match seems almost transcendentally ludicrous when recounted in a single paragraph like that, but if we take a look at the context, it somehow becomes even sillier still. The odds of that must be, what, 500 to 1?

The most obviously significant recent event was that Botham had just been sacked as England captain.

Or had he? Botham had been serving as England captain on a kind of zero hours contract – one match at a time, with no guarantee of future work. The second Test of the series had been his 12th and last in charge, eight of which ended up draws and four of which were defeats.

One of the most significant contributors to this woeful record had been a perfectly dreadful cricketer known as Ian Botham.

When first named captain in June 1980, Beefy had boasted a Test batting average of 40.48 after 25 Tests and had hit six hundreds. His bowling average had been 18.52 and he had taken no fewer than 14 five-wicket hauls. The man was shaping up to be not merely one of the best players of all time, but quite possibly two of them.

However, over those next dozen Tests, he transformed into one player – and a decidedly mediocre one at that. In that period he averaged 13.14 with the bat with just one fifty, and took 35 wickets at the meh-to-poor average of 33.08. In his final match in charge, he made a three-ball duck in the first innings. While the odds of doing even worse than that in the second innings must have been, what, 500 to 1, he nevertheless managed it, getting bowled behind his legs by the first ball to secure a most ignominious pair.

Enough was enough, concluded someone – or quite possibly everyone (it wasn't entirely clear).

In the TV highlights from the time, Richie Benaud said that Botham immediately went to the selectors after the match and asked to be made captain for the rest of the series. According to Richie, they said no because they were sacking him. That was one version. Botham wrote in his autobiography that he had decided to resign after the game and claimed that was what he went to speak to the selectors about. That was another version. Finally, the chairman of selection, Alec Bedser, said that Botham had asked to be allowed to say he had resigned – but Bedser also made it 100 per cent clear that he had wanted to sack him as captain anyway.

While the truth was hard to discern, two things were clear: Botham was no longer captain, and Bedser was kind of a tool.

So it was that Botham entered the Headingley Test not just crestfallen and humiliated, but also possessed of a bowling average across his last dozen Tests that was inferior to the future career records of Dermot Reeve and Andy Bichel. Even more damningly, his batting average in that period was also inferior to those same two players.

However, Ian Botham being Ian Botham, he promptly took a wicket with his third ball and finished with figures of 6/95 in Australia's first innings.

If he were under any illusions that his teammates might lend a hand when England replied, he was swiftly disabused of them. His 50 was more than twice as many runs as the next best effort – David Gower's silky[1] 24.

The follow-on innings went a little better, in that Graham Dilley made 56, batting at number nine. That was the only other England half-century, though.

When Botham then opened the bowling and dismissed Graeme Wood, he had at that point in the match taken seven of England's ten wickets and scored 199 of their 530 runs.

This set things up for Bob Willis – who had taken 0/72 in the first innings, having bowled the small matter of 28 no balls in an innings in the previous Test (in one innings, that

---

1   It wasn't actually silky at all, but it's de rigueur to describe all David Gower innings with that word.

is, not in the match) – to take 8/43 and win the Test.

The key to this bowling turnaround was apparently a simply outlandish gambit from England's new captain, Mike Brearley, who had told Willis not to worry about no balls. (You're defending 130 and your fast bowler's been overstepping 28 times an innings and you're saying you're not bothered about no balls? Good one, Mike – very convincing.)

Botham wasn't done yet, though. Headingley had merely levelled the series at 1–1. More heroics would be needed for England to win the Ashes. In the fourth Test, England set Australia 151 to win. Scores hadn't been high, but Brearley felt it had been a good pitch throughout and that England had thrown wickets away 'gratuitously' in their first innings.

This seemed a decent assessment when Australia reached 4/105, putting them just 46 runs from victory. At this point John Emburey got Allan Border for 40 off 175 balls (wickets were falling very rarely) and Brearley brought Botham on.

Botham had been reluctant to bowl until this point because the pitch wasn't doing anything and he didn't see how he could get anyone out. There's a story that he wasn't even going to put his bowling boots on at the start of the session until Brearley instructed him to. (More than most series, the 1981 Ashes generates weird little side stories. It's as if this particular series is so mythic it spawns bonus material, like the Star Wars book *Tales from the Mos Eisley Cantina*.)

Botham then took 5/1 in 28 balls and England won by 29 runs.

In the fifth Test, England were labouring in their second innings to the extent that when Botham came in, Geoffrey Boycott boasted the highest strike rate of the six batters who'd been to the crease, thanks to his caution-to-the-wind knock of 37 runs off 122 balls. (The odds of that must have been, what, 500 to 1?)

Boycott was joined by Chris Tavaré for one particularly stultifying partnership. It would be going too far to claim that Boycott was the hare to Tavaré's tortoise. It would probably be more accurate to say he was the tortoise to Tavaré's pharmaceutically nobbled tortoise.

The latter, who was still at the crease when Botham came in, at one point scored all of 11 runs in a session. But while Botham's arrival, batting at number seven, triggered only further inaction from Tavaré, the man himself shrugged off a golden duck in the first innings to make 118 off 102 balls. Having come in at number three, Tavaré continued afterwards, and when he was finally out after seven hours of batting, he was still 40 runs shy of what Botham had managed in two.

Australia needed 506 to win, and they got closer than you'd think – all out for 402.

The 1981 Ashes was so ridiculous, it even featured a sixth Test. By this point Botham was running on fumes, trundling in innocuously to bowl rank medium pace. He took ten wickets.

3

STUART BROAD SMASHES ONE TO SLIP

AKA THESE BOOS WEREN'T MADE FOR WALKING

Stuart Broad fielding in front of the small group of Brisbane fans who at least have the common decency to use his name.

If you've read this far into this book, you've probably noticed that Stuart Christopher John Broad is one of the great purveyors of ridiculousness in Ashes history.

To recap just a handful of examples of his top-tier nonsense, Broad picked a fight with an Australian boundary rider robot in Hobart in 2022, aborting his run-up after being distracted by the little fella and yelling, 'Stop moving the robot!' Earlier in that series, he secured a draw alongside Jimmy Anderson, as England's all-time top two duck-makers batted out the last couple of overs in Sydney.[1] Broad later unilaterally declared the Covid-impacted series void. Because of course he did.

In 2015, at Trent Bridge, Broad bowled one of the maddest spells in Ashes history, securing a series win in the opening session of a Test (see No. 17). He finished with 8/15 that morning, and reacted to a Ben Stokes catch with the instantly memeworthy 'Broadface', a wide-eyed, mouth-covering, *Home Alone*–movie poster gasp of amazement.

Broad was also the man who showed up in the middle following Jonny Bairstow's stumping in 2023 (see No. 8). He immediately fanned the flames, trolling the Australians with exaggerated groundings of his bat behind the crease and mock innocent clarifications at the end of each over about whether it was reasonable to now consider the ball dead. He wound up his career later that series by popularising a previously obscure (and perhaps non-existent) cricketing superstition, switching the bails in order to capture a match-winning, series-levelling wicket (see No. 23).

It's a tremendous body of work, easily enough to secure his standing as a titan of cricketing absurdity.

But we haven't even mentioned the big one yet, have we? Let's rectify that.

In the first Test of the 2013 Ashes, Australia led by 65 on the first innings, thanks to the heroics of Ashton Agar (see No. 14). Broad arrived at the crease in the second innings to join Ian Bell at 6/218, a lead of 153. The pair added 79 runs before Agar caught the top edge of Broad's bat as he played back and attempted an optimistic late-cut variant. The ball clipped Brad Haddin's

---

[1] Wonderfully, Anderson's final moment in Ashes cricket in Australia was him blocking out an over of leg-spin from Steve Smith. Two all-time legends of the game deciding a match using their wrong skill sets. What a mad and brilliant sport. But let's not get distracted.

gloves and flew to Michael Clarke at first slip.

Clarke threw the ball in the air in delight. Haddin clapped his gloves together. Agar leapt and smiled.

And Stuart Broad, heroically, ridiculously, stood his ground.

Umpire Aleem Dar bizarrely gave Broad not out and Australia, having burnt all their reviews on some nonsense or other, were left with no recourse.

In the moment, the Australian team took the decision more or less in their stride. Clarke chewed his gum a little harder. Occasional frowns of confusion were spotted. But overall, it was a measured reaction to such a dreadful decision. If they were New Zealand, they might have even won a Spirit of Cricket award for their response.

At the close of play, a far-too-reasonable Peter Siddle offered the following thoughts on the incident: 'How many people have ever walked? Some. That's right, some.' He went on to add that 'obviously people are going to be frustrated but it's hard out there for players, for umpires. It's a long day, it's a tough day for people out there.

Things are going to happen and we just have to deal with it.'

Later, things got more heated. Probably around the point when Australia lost the Test by 14 runs, and the ramifications of the extra 59 runs Broad added after refusing to walk became clearer. (In a perfect piece of storytelling, the Test ended with Haddin edging the ball through to the keeper: he was given not out, only for England to have a review remaining. After Alastair Cook sent the decision upstairs, Haddin admitted to the England team he'd nicked it.[2] So they all stood around waiting to see if the technology would detect the edge. It did.)

Australia lost the 2013 Ashes 3–0, then faced England again a few months later in the return 2013/14 series.

By that point, Broad's refusal to walk had been hypocritically reimagined by sections of the Australian media as one of the most heinous crimes in Ashes history. Leading the crusade was a Brisbane tabloid newspaper, *The Courier-Mail*, which, for unclear reasons, declared that they were not going to call Broad by his name. They instead referred to

---

2   'How many people have ever walked? Some. That's right, some.'

him by the Voldemortian '27-year-old English medium pacer'.

Naturally, Broad leant into the absurdity of all this drama. He took five wickets on the first day of the series and strolled into the press conference at the close of play with a copy of *The Courier-Mail* under his arm. Wonderful stuff. (The next day the newspaper referred to him as a 'Phantom Menace', which is definitely an insult too far.)

That first day, however, was the only day of the series in which England were on top. On the second day, they lost 6/9 as they were bowled out for 136 (last man out: Broad, 32 runs from 45 balls), as Mitchell Johnson arrived in the series. England never regained parity.

Johnson finished with figures of 4/61 and 5/42 (and scores of 64 and 39 not out) in the first Test. Then, in the first innings of the second Test, he took 7/40, the highlight of which, naturally, was the dismissal of Broad.

The wicket came in his 14th over, a triple-wicket maiden and one of the finest nonsense overs in Ashes history.

With his first ball, Johnson hit a young Ben Stokes on the pad. Stokes was given not out but wandered out of his crease. The underarm throw at the stumps from gully missed and went for four overthrows, which were signalled as coming off the bat. Clarke, convinced Stokes hadn't hit it, reviewed the decision and it came back as out LBW – also negating the overthrows.

The next four balls saw Johnson work Matt Prior over, before he had him caught behind for a duck. Which brought in Stuart Broad.

Now, Adelaide Oval at the time was not widely thought of as a volatile cauldron bubbling over with fired-up fans. 'Picturesque' was the adjective more commonly employed to describe it. But with Johnson bowling thunderbolts, the Adelaide crowd was baying for Broad's blood. Baying picturesquely.

Broad arrived at the crease with sunscreen on his nose – in itself a tremendously silly show of confidence, given the carnage that Johnson was wreaking. But Broad, the peerless showman, knew what he was doing. The zinc cream was actually an excellent example of sunsmartness from Broad. For, rather than face up to Johnson, he instead spent many, many minutes adjusting the sightscreen. So many minutes, in fact, that Channel Nine changed commentary teams in between him arriving at the crease and receiving his first ball.

The sightscreen issue was caused by light glinting off some metal component. In Australia, in 2013/14, the sun itself was anti–Stuart Broad. No wonder he was wearing sunscreen.

Eventually, however, after much gesticulation and many adjustments, Broad was left with no choice but to face up to Johnson. Brilliantly, he was bowled first ball, walking past a delivery that crashed into his leg stump. Adelaide roared and Johnson zoomed off, arms wide in celebration. Broad practised his leg glance and then took another look at his leg stump, almost visibly trying to work out the geometry.

As the old saying goes, 'Revenge is a dish best served first ball at Adelaide Oval after a lengthy sightscreen delay.'

Australia's towering, ridiculous enemy had been (momentarily) vanquished – but not before his departure was accompanied by one last piece of superb nonsense.

Because as Broad trudged off, the graphic accompanying him read 'Stuart Broad, 0, 1 ball, 1 minute', in total denial of the actual length of time he'd been out in the middle, mucking about. Even in making a comical golden duck, the great man had up-ended everything we take for granted in cricket.

Stuart Christopher John Broad – how many other Ashes cricketers have ever been this ridiculous? None. That's right, none.

2

GERAINT JONES CATCHES MICHAEL KASPROWICZ

AKA ALL YOU NEED IS GLOVE

The 2005 Ashes is regarded by many people as the greatest series of all time. Who can forget the spectacular climax when two officials ostentatiously carried out some kind of bail-removal, stump-withdrawal ceremony because it was a bit cloudy and probably wasn't going to get any less cloudy before the scheduled close of play?

Okay, maybe that was the official end of the series and not in fact the 'climax', in the dramatic sense. For all the splendour of Kevin Pietersen's caution-to-the-wind 158 – when he responded to an England collapse and the apparent inevitability of his dismissal to Brett Lee by hooking a series of heart-in-mouth sixes – maybe the 2005 Ashes climax in fact came long before the fifth Test at the Oval.

As mad as it sounds, the climax of the 2005 Ashes, really, was the end of the second Test, at Edgbaston – because that's when emotions peaked.

Emotions peaked then because jeopardy peaked then. It wasn't just the outcome of the Test match that was at stake when Steve Harmison ran in to bowl the final ball to Michael Kasprowicz. The likely outcome of the series was at stake too, and therefore also the ongoing and total dominance of the Australia team, which at that moment stretched all the way back to Australia's 1989 Ashes series victory.

England hadn't just been beaten since then. They had been cracked, beaten and whisked into a froth, before being baked, devoured and deposited into a porcelain tomb. Even when it hadn't seemed possible, things had just carried on getting worse and worse for them.

The previous series, Down Under, had ended 4–1 in Australia's favour, with two innings victories and another that was equally resounding.[1] A little further back, the last Test the two teams had played on English shores – the last of the 2001 series – had seen Australia declare their only innings on 4/641. Usman Afzaal had been the pick of England's bowlers, the middle-order batter having taken the highest-profile of his 98 first-class wickets (Adam Gilchrist for 25) to finish with figures of 1/49 off nine overs. Glenn McGrath then took a five-for and Shane Warne 11 wickets in the match as Australia secured another of those increasingly routine innings victories.

---

1   England were bowled out for 79 when chasing 464 to win.

The one thing you could say from England's perspective was that there was certainly room for improvement.

And they did improve. Not just to the point where they were no longer batting twice as many times as their opponents, but to the point where they were actually defeating them. In the home summer of 2004, they won all seven Tests – three against New Zealand and four against the West Indies.

Far and away the best Test side in the world, Australia didn't take these results too seriously; psychologically maimed long-term England supporters were similarly reluctant to get their hopes up.

But hope got harder to suppress when the 2005 tour got underway. England won the T20 international by 100 runs through devious employment of the futuristic tactic of 'taking the format seriously'. There then followed not one but two series of ODIs: the NatWest Series – a tri-series that also involved Bangladesh – and the Bangladesh-free NatWest Challenge.

In the first NatWest Series match, Steve Harmison dismissed Adam Gilchrist, Matthew Hayden, Ricky Ponting, Damien Martyn and Mike Hussey (not the worst five-for in the world) to finish with 5/33. Kevin Pietersen then hit 91 off 65 balls to complete the run chase.

In the final, England fell to 5/33 while chasing, but Paul Collingwood and Geraint Jones rescued the innings and the match ended in a tie. The NatWest Challenge therefore shaped up as a three-match Super Over, which Australia won 2–1.

Nevertheless, England had shown they were up for a fight and there was much excitement ahead of the first morning of the first Test at Lord's. This escalated when Harmison literally drew blood, cutting Ponting's cheek, having already hit both Hayden and Justin Langer.

Harmison's 5/43 helped hustle Australia out for 190, inflating a gigantic balloon of English optimism that hovered ominously over the hallowed ground's sloping outfield. But wait! Who was this lanky figure, striding to his mark armed with a metaphorical pin? It was that arch English-Balloon-of-Hopefulness-popper, Glenn McGrath, who duly showered the crowd with rubbery shreds by taking 5/7.

If Australia all out for 190 felt like England had taken a train to Bizarro World, then slumping to 5/21 in reply suggested they'd fallen asleep at some point and inadvertently made the return journey after the train had set off back again.

Australia won by 239 runs and, despite some conspicuously wilful disrespect for McGrath and Warne from Pietersen, English hope was again in abeyance.

That lasted until about lunch on the first day of the second Test at Edgbaston, by which point Marcus Trescothick was already on 77.

Ponting had won the toss. Perhaps forgetting that his match-winning opening bowler had just been taken to hospital after treading on a ball during the warm-ups, he decided to have a bowl. For some reason, no one thought to question Trescothick's pace-making and England finished the day 407 all out – no mean feat, given they'd failed to pass 180 in either innings in the first Test.

Their efforts ultimately resulted in a 99-run first innings lead. They then took this advantage, screwed it up in a ball and dropped it in the recycling bin: 4/31 became 6/75 before Andrew Flintoff – fresh from taking two wickets in two balls to finish Australia's first innings – walloped 73 to set Australia 282 to win.

This was obviously too many. Except that obviousness began to melt away.

At 0/47 and with the crowd flatter than an ironed pancake, Michael Vaughan remembered that Flintoff was on a hat-trick and brought him on to bowl. The ridiculousness of the over that followed can only be appreciated in that context.

The devil of defeatism was never far from English shoulders during this period. Australia had spent almost two full decades reliably dashing optimism, the first Test had gone totally awry, and Ashley Giles had just conceded seven runs in a third over that was every bit as inconsequential and nondescript as his first two.

And then suddenly Flintoff crashed in, like a big cartoon genie.

The hat-trick ball was, arguably, the least exciting. Langer then elbowed the second into his stumps, which gave Ponting the opportunity to endure a torrid few deliveries. Repeatedly beaten, he survived two LBW shouts before edging the final ball to wicketkeeper Jones.

It was an immaculate punctuation mark on a stupendous over. *That's how you do a climax*, we all thought. But no, actually ... it turns out sporting climaxes can be a lot more emotionally charged than that.

Australia folded to 8/175 at the close of play and England had basically

Steve Harmison and Michael Kasprowicz enjoy a carefree moment of cricket with little riding on it.

won. Hadn't they? Obviously, there was a little bit of reticence in the English chicken-counting, given the previous decade and a half of Ashes cricket, but 107 runs from the last two wickets? It just doesn't happen in the fourth innings of a Test match.

Shane Warne, however, was not like other cricketers, while it's been established earlier in this book (see No. 25) that Brett Lee was the man you'd pick to bat for your life. These were the two men at the crease.

Like Flintoff, Warne was on a roll. He'd taken 6/46 in England's second innings, including a ludicrous pastiche of his own Ball of the (Previous) Century to dismiss Andrew Strauss. Those efforts brought to the fore England's deep-rooted suspicion that maybe this wasn't their story; that maybe Warne was John Wick and they were merely his cannon fodder.[2]

Warne exploited this dynamic to move the score to 8/220, before inexplicably, catastrophically, backheeling his own stumps.[3]

English tension briefly dissipated before slowly escalating to a point beyond which every subsequent step represented the greatest sporting tension ever felt. Because where other sports can give you five minutes of anxiety at the very end and the odd moment within that where something meaningful might happen, Test cricket can give you an hour of excruciating suffering, with every single delivery the equivalent of a 'chance'. Lee and Kasprowicz got Australia within three runs of victory – and they didn't get there quickly.

Not to labour the point here, but England had lost matches to Australia before. They had, in fact, got pretty good at it over the course of eight successive Ashes series defeats. This one would have been different, though. This would have been not just defeat from the jaws of victory, but a humiliation beyond words – a new and defining example of deal-sealing inability.

As Harmison ran in to bowl to Kasprowicz with Australia one shot from victory, everything was at stake.

---

2   This wasn't a literal thought, obviously, given that *John Wick* didn't come into existence for another decade.
3   Is this the one and only difference between Warne and John Wick? That the latter would never accidentally tread on his own stumps during a tight Ashes run chase? Who can say? Possibly there's some other stuff too.

The match, most obviously – the helter-skelter first innings and Flintoff's superhuman day – and the summer-long build-up too, spanning all those one-day matches. More broadly, the England side's newfound willingness to go toe-to-toe with Australia was at stake, along with everything that represented.

On-field resurgence had given birth to a (hugely reluctant) willingness to dream that, after sixteen long years, things could finally be different. But if Kasprowicz were to edge this one for four, things wouldn't be different. Not really. If anything, they would be an even worse version of the same, if you can overlook the inherent contradiction of that statement. Australia would be 2–0 up and England's ability to win a Test match from even the most dominant position would be shot.

Eight Ashes series defeats in a row would be nine and counting. One fluky boundary and it basically felt like England would never win again.

Can the climax of a five-Test series really come in the second match? Given that the tension had been building since Australia took the Ashes in 1989, and that it could potentially now break one way or the exact opposite way based on the outcome of a single ball ... Yeah, this was the climax.

Harmison pitched it short. Kasprowicz recoiled. Jones dived. Emotions were felt.

The fact that Kasprowicz's hand wasn't even on the bat was somehow both irrelevant and also the preposterous cherry on this supernaturally ridiculous cake.

1

SHANE WARNE SHOWS UP

AKA GATT'S BALL, FOLKS!

Mike Gatting recalibrates his mental protractor.

Where were you for Shane Warne's first ball in Ashes cricket? Maybe you aren't old enough to have seen it live or on the highlights at the time. In that case, what do you know of it? Warne went on to become such a colossally significant figure in the context of this contest that it's quite the historic moment – the kind of thing you can expect to stumble on when being buffeted about on the choppy seas of the YouTube algorithm.

Just in case you're a miraculous Venn diagram intersection of a person who has both a) willingly persevered this far into a cricket book centred around the highlights of the last fifty years of the Ashes, and b) somehow avoided all knowledge of Warne's first Ashes ball, here's a quick rundown.

Facing the bowling of Phil Tufnell, Warne, batting at number nine, played well back and defended with a straight bat for no run.

You, the reader of this book, are now, no doubt, shaking your head in blinking confusion and raising your eyebrows in surprise. You thought you knew where we were going with that opening paragraph. Then carefully followed the trajectory of the topic into the second paragraph, despite it swerving quite alarmingly away from its initial line and into Venn diagram chat.

Then came the sudden turn of the third paragraph. Defying your expectations. Ripping past your reading comprehension defences. Defences you perhaps didn't even think you needed to put up. Who in blue blazes writes about the first ball Warne *faced* in Ashes cricket?

Answer: we, the co-authors of this book, do. And we're now embracing in delight at having got one past you. Maybe even throwing an unnecessary farewell sledge at you.

(Cue understated Richie Benaud commentary: 'And they've done it.')

Look, sorry to Gatting you in such a cruel fashion, but it was necessary to provide a fresh appreciation of the moment we're actually discussing here. The first ball Shane Warne *bowled* in Ashes cricket. The, you know, Ball of the Century.

It's a moment now so firmly embedded in cricket history that the full scale of how ridiculous it was can be overlooked.

Australia had brought a leg-spinner with them on their previous Ashes tour in 1989. That leg-spinner was future selectorial nemesis of Steve Waugh, Trevor Hohns (see No. 32). Hohns played five of the six Tests on that 1989 tour, taking 11 wickets at an average of 27.27, with best figures of 3/59. That three-wicket effort came in the fourth Test at Old Trafford and featured a flipper that deceived David Gower, LBW for 35. Gower's dismissal was followed an over later by the wicket of Ian Botham, unluckily bowled after advancing down the pitch and wildly swinging in an attempt to hit the ball into the Headingley confectionery stand, 70 kilometres away.

Eleven wickets from five Tests with very occasional smatterings of satisfying wicket-taking deception was more or less all one could reasonably expect from leg-spinners in this era. (Notable exception: Abdul Qadir of Pakistan, who was pretty much the only consistently successful purveyor of the wrist-spinning arts through the 1980s.[1])

When Allan Border tossed the ball to Shane Warne in 1993, then, England had no real reason to suspect what would happen next.

Warne had played eleven Tests in the eighteen months since he'd debuted against India with bowling figures of 1/150. He'd taken just 31 wickets in those eleven Tests. Nevertheless, he had also conjured a few noteworthy spells.

In his third Test, he'd saved Australia from a humiliating first ever Test defeat against the easybeats of world cricket at the time, Sri Lanka. With career bowling figures of 1/335 when he was thrown the ball, Warne took 3/11 to bowl Sri Lanka out for 164 as they chased 181 for victory.

A couple of Tests later, back on Australian soil and facing the hardbeats of world cricket at the time, the West Indies, Warne spun Australia to victory once more. He once again improved his best figures, this time to 7/52, including a famous flipper that bamboozled Richie Richardson when the visitors were motoring at 1/143 in pursuit of their 359 victory target.

So England had enough information to suggest that Warne was perhaps a slightly better bowler than Hohns. Potentially a hurdle to overcome in a fourth-innings run chase.

There was definitely no intel, however, that he would bowl England's best player of spin bowling with his very first delivery. Or that the ball would be a snaking reimagination of everything previously understood

---

1 To the extent that in 1987 he was asked to bowl 73 of Pakistan's 148 overs across England's two innings in Lahore. (Spoilsport Mudassar Nazar bowled a one-over opening spell in the second innings.)

about feasible paths by which a cricket ball might traverse the twenty-two yards of a pitch (or, indeed, further than twenty-two yards, given its improbable route).

From Warne's hand, the ball headed leg-sideish, before disconcertingly swerving still further in that direction. Touching down well outside Gatting's leg stump, on a good length, it then zipped back with diabolical sharpness, past his straight-batted defensive shot to hit the top of off stump (just above one of those new-fangled stump cameras, which would forever more, on every fresh rewatch of this most rewatched of deliveries, reward the rewatcher with a startling close-up view of Gatting's enormous posterior).

Gatting's reaction is almost as iconic as the delivery itself. He glances back at the stumps, trying to make sense of how, exactly, they've been broken. Then the raised eyebrows of surprise and slow glove removal as he accepts the mind-bending reality that he has somehow been bowled.

Gatting was correct to be shell-shocked by what had happened to him. It was a hell of a delivery. The most emphatic entrance to the Ashes anybody had ever made (and eliciting one of the more comically stunned exits).

Having made that entrance, Warne settled in and made himself at home.

He kicked off his shoes and ripped another delivery, taking the outside edge of Robin Smith's bat, safely pouched by Mark Taylor at slip. He helped himself to a beer from the fridge and had Graham Gooch caught at mid-on from a full toss. He settled in on the couch for the afternoon and took five more wickets in the Test (Andy Caddick, Mike Atherton, Alec Stewart, Chris Lewis and Robin Smith again).[2]

'Is it okay if I just crash here for a few days?' Warne then asked, as he went on to become the top wicket-taker for the series, with 34 at 25.79.

Like the most annoying cousin Eddie in the world, those few days turned into fourteen years of the leg-spinner making an absolute thundering nuisance of himself against England.

Even watching on TV, Warne always gave England fans heart

---

2   Gooch, sensibly, would be out handling the ball in the second innings, flicking it away before it could bounce onto his stumps. Which is definitely one way to avoid humiliation by leg break.

palpitations. If their team required 12 runs to win and still had all ten wickets in hand, when Warne was bowling they would still feel Australia were favourites.

Meanwhile, on the field, batting paralysis frequently arose from the same emotional response, which meant it often seemed like run-scoring was a physical impossibility and that the fall of a wicket was only ever a ball away (see No. 7).

With all due respect to Stuart Broad, Steve Smith, Ian Botham, Steve Waugh, Ben Stokes and the other usual ridiculous suspects of the last half-century of Ashes cricket that we've covered in this book, there's nobody who pulled off quite the same volume of ridiculous Ashes nonsense as Shane Warne.

Ridiculous Ashes bowler.
Ridiculous Ashes career.

Right from the very first ball (that he bowled).

ACKNOWLEDGEMENTS

Alex and Dan would like to thank Affirm, for all the obvious reasons that authors thank publishers (the work involved from multiple parties to convert all these words into physical form and make it available to people to read is not to be underestimated); the women who first burnt and presented the Ashes, as well as Reginald Shirley Brooks for that 1882 mock obituary in *The Sporting Times*; Dave Tickner and *Cricket365* for first letting us write ridiculous Ashes stuff together; all the broadcasters and reporters who do the serious day-to-day legwork of covering the game; and cricketers in general and Pat Cummins in particular.

Alex would also like to thank Neal Anthwal for saying, 'You should write – people do that, you know'; Edward Craig for emailing about the word 'embiggen' that time; the *King Cricket* readers for all the years of support (and comments); and Rob Williams for making the writing of books seem not wholly unreasonable.

Closer to home, he would like to thank Sian, Niamh and Owen for tolerating the empty presence of a man whose mind is often away at Trent Bridge or the Gabba or somewhere. He would also like to thank Dan for writing the other half of this book during the night-time, like some sort of benevolent, nocturnal, literary auto-complete gremlin.

Dan would like to thank Cat, who remains the number one supporter of his writing; his mother, who was the predecessor in that role and encouraged him in the writing caper when all the smart money was that he should be a computer nerd; his father, whose bookshelf consists solely of Dan's books; and the online supporters who subscribe to read his regular musings (plug: newsletter.liebcricket.com!). And, of course, thanks to Alex, a fine benevolent, nocturnal, literary auto-complete gremlin in his own right, and one with whom it's been a pleasure to collaborate.

IMAGE CREDITS

Pages 6–7: Laurence Griffiths/PA Images/Alamy Stock Photo

Page 11: Phil Hillyard/Newspix

Page 17: News Images Ltd/Alamy Stock Photo

Page 23: Einstock/Alamy Stock Vector

Pages 32–3: PA Images/Alamy Stock Photo

Page 35: Tony Henshaw/Alamy Stock Photo

Page 41: Goddard Archive/Alamy Stock Photo

Page 47: News Ltd/Newspix

Page 53: s&g/PA Images/Alamy Stock Photo

Page 59: ZUMA Press/Alamy Stock Photo

Page 65: Anthony Devlin/PA Images/Alamy Stock Photo

Pages 72–3: Rebecca Naden/PA Images/Alamy Stock Photo

Pages 80–1: Cal Sport Media/Alamy Stock Photo

Page 83: EMPICS/PA Images/Alamy Stock Photo

Page 89: Jason O'Brien/PA Images/Alamy Stock Photo

Pages 96–7: Neal Simpson/PA Images/Alamy Stock Photo

Page 101: S.Bent/PA Images/Alamy Stock Photo

Page 107: Mark Kerton/PA Images/Alamy Stock Photo

Page 113: Phil Walter/PA Images/Alamy Stock Photo

Page 119: Jason O'Brien/PA Images/Alamy Stock Photo

Page 125: News Ltd/Newspix

Page 131: Gareth Copley/PA Images/Alamy Stock Photo

Pages 140–1: Steven Paston/PA Images/Alamy Stock Photo

Pages 146–7: Phil Walter/PA Images/Alamy Stock Photo

Pages 152–3: Dave Hewison/Speed Media/Alamy Stock Photo

Page 155: Allstar Picture Library/Alamy Stock Photo

Page 161: Ross Setford/PA Images/Alamy Stock Photo

Pages 168–9: Mike Egerton/PA Images/Alamy Stock Photo

Page 173: EMPICS Sport/PA Images/Alamy Stock Photo

IMAGE CREDITS

Pages 180–1: Brendan Monks/PA Images/Alamy Stock Photo

Pages 186–7: Mike Egerton/PA Images/Alamy Stock Photo

Pages 194–5: Chris Ison/PA Images/Alamy Stock Photo

Pages 198–9: Phil Walter/PA Images/Alamy Stock Photo

Pages 206–7: Mike Egerton/PA Images/Alamy Stock Photo

Page 209: Glenn Barnes/Newspix

Pages 216–7: Harris/PA Images/Alamy Stock Photo

Page 221: Rui Vieira/PA Images/Alamy Stock Photo

Page 227: Rui Vieira/PA Images/Alamy Stock Photo

Pages 234–5: Sport and General/PA Images/Alamy Stock Photo

Page 239: Gareth Copley/PA Images/Alamy Stock Photo

Page 245: Gareth Fuller/PA Images/Alamy Stock Photo

Page 251: Nick Potts/PA Images/Alamy Stock Photo

Page 257: Adam Davy/PA Images/Alamy Stock Photo

Page 263: Gareth Copley/PA Images/Alamy Stock Photo

Page 269: Anthony Devlin/PA Images/Alamy Stock Photo

Pages 278–9: Tim Goode/PA Images/Alamy Stock Photo

Page 283: PA Images/Alamy Stock Photo

Page 289: Anthony Devlin/PA Images/Alamy Stock Photo

Pages 298–9: David Ashdown/Independent/Alamy Stock Photo

Page 303: PA Images/Alamy Stock Photo

Back cover (left): EMPICS Sport/PA Images/Alamy Stock Photo

Back cover (middle): News Ltd/Newspix

Back cover (right): Anthony Devlin/PA Images/Alamy Stock Photo